Excuse Me, Your Life Is Waiting!

A Bridge from Addiction to Early Recovery

Robert Boich

iUniverse, Inc.
New York   Bloomington

Excuse Me, Your Life Is Waiting!
A Bridge from Addiction to Early Recovery

iUniverse books may be ordered through booksellers or by contacting:

iUniverse
1663 Liberty Drive
Bloomington, IN 47403
www.iuniverse.com
1-800-Authors (1-800-288-4677)

Because of the dynamic nature of the Internet, any Web addresses or links contained in this book may have changed since publication and may no longer be valid. The views expressed in this work are solely those of the author and do not necessarily reflect the views of the publisher, and the publisher hereby disclaims any responsibility for them.

ISBN: 978-1-4401-2105-0 (sc)
ISBN: 978-1-4401-2107-4 (dj)
ISBN: 978-1-4401-2106-7 (ebook)

Library of Congress Control Number: 2009925173

Printed in the United States of America

iUniverse rev. date: 3/23/2009

This book is dedicated to my wife, who led the way, and to my parents, who have always been behind me.

Contents

Introduction

This story is about change. It's about shedding old ideas and habits in exchange for a new way of thinking and a different approach to life. It's personal in nature—at least it's personal to me. It's really the only story I'm qualified to tell. It's my story, and I'm going to share it with you for a very simple reason. I want to help.

I started writing a couple of months before the book idea came up. It really wasn't a story at first. It was a journal, a combination of thoughts and feelings on my life and the world around me. I originally had no plans of sharing it with anyone. The idea for this project came from one of my counselors. He encouraged me to write this book.

I'm not sure what prompted me to start keeping a written record in the first place. I tried it once before, at my first rehab. It was supposed to be part of the recovery process. I think I may have written a couple of pages. I probably didn't stick with it, because at that point in my life, I had no real intention of getting clean. About the most I could muster at the time was the notion that it might be a good idea to cut back a little. I just wasn't ready.

My life was spiraling out of control. I had to do something. I wasn't exactly sure what, but I was going to have to make some changes if I wanted to keep my family. My wife was going back to rehab. She was embroiled in a custody battle over her daughter, and things weren't going well. Children's services and the local police had recently made a surprise visit to our residence to check on our young son. On top of that, one of our friends had committed suicide the same day, after leaving our house. This was in addition to the usual, garden-variety, negative consequences that alcoholics and addicts are faced with on a daily basis: family problems, financial trouble, health issues, and legal predicaments.

Given the state of my affairs, any rational person would realize that something was wrong. Not me; I couldn't make the connection. I still entertained the idea that I would be able to control my drug and alcohol use. All I needed was a little time off. My plan was to go away for a while, get cleaned up, and approach things in a little more structured manner. Unlike my wife, I had no intentions of going back to rehab. What could they possibly tell me that I hadn't heard at my first treatment facility? I was going to do it on my own. I thought I would still be able to drink and drug on occasion. I was just going to tone things down a bit. I decided to go to Europe when my wife went back into rehab. I just needed some time alone to sort things out. I could get away from everything and reflect—reflect and write. That's how I began to keep a journal.

As far as my recovery goes, I made a few discoveries while I was overseas. I began to realize how my behavior had been affecting my family: children, parents, siblings, and my wife. It was a difficult time. It allowed me to see enough of myself to realize that I had a problem, but it fell short of providing me with any answers that would help me with my sobriety. Still, it was a start.

I had promised my wife that I would enroll in an outpatient program when I got back from Europe. I really didn't want to, but I felt I had to. At the time, I thought abstinence and sobriety were synonymous. I was so messed up. I didn't know where I was headed or what I was going to do. As you'll see, this all changed shortly after I got back to the States. I started attending twelve-step meetings, and I got myself into a six-week outpatient program. All the while, I kept writing.

I offer you this background to give you an idea of where I was and what my life was like. These are the events that got me to where I am today. Keep in mind, I'm not trying to tell anyone what to do. I can only share what has worked for me. There's nothing original about my program of recovery. I am merely relaying what others have passed on to me. I take no credit for the actual tools involved. Many of them are concepts that have been around for quite some time.

One of the first things I learned was that I was looking at things backwards: fix my substance abuse problems, and my life would fix itself. It seemed to make sense at the time. It goes back to the abstinence versus sobriety issue I mentioned earlier. It's true, abstinence definitely improved my life. I could see a difference in myself after a couple of weeks. The problem with this approach is that I was still the same person. I had to look at the bigger picture. One of my new friends explained it to me like this: "The man I was drank. The man I was will drink again. I have to change the man." That statement echoed the sentiments of one of my counselors, the same one who encouraged me to write this book. He told me that in order to stay sober, I had to change only one thing. Everything!

Any illusions I might have had about finding a quick solution to my problems had disappeared. In the past, I would've just said, *Screw it. I can fix this on my own.* The problem was, I couldn't. My way wasn't working, and it hadn't worked in a long time. I surrendered, at least temporarily. What could it hurt? I figured anything was worth a try. I could always go back to my old way of life. I threw myself into recovery: meetings and readings, new friends and new ideas. I asked a lot of questions, but more importantly, I listened to the answers. I spent several hours a day going to meetings and writing about the topics that were discussed. I applied the lessons I was learning to my everyday life and recorded my experiences in my journal. I also started writing essays on an assortment of topics. Most of these were related to recovery, while others were merely personal observations on life in general.

The story you are about to read is a combination of these observations and my experiences during the first six months of sobriety. I've tried to present these materials in a manner that anyone fresh in recovery can easily understand. If you've come this far, I hope my experiences will convince you to keep going. There is a wonderful world out there in sobriety, a way of life far more rewarding than anything I'd ever known. It's not easy, but it's not nearly as difficult as I thought it would be, either. Believe me when I tell you, if I can do it, so can you. Just don't try to do it by yourself. There's a lot of help out there, people who have been where you are now and who are willing to help you find a better way. Good luck!

Personal Itinerary

Who we are is a manifestation of where we've been and what we've done. It's these life travels and experiences that make up our person. On its face, this may appear to be a simple concept, one about which most people would probably say, "Sure, makes sense—experience, there's no substitute for it." But it becomes more difficult for some individuals to grasp and accept this concept when negative or destructive actions and consequences are thrown into the mix.

We struggle with our past, instead of accepting the things we've done. How many times have we said to ourselves, "I wish I had done that differently," or "Wouldn't my life be different if only that hadn't happened to me?" Yes, things would be different. Our lives would be changed. We wouldn't be the same people we are at this very moment. For better or for worse, our personal makeup would be altered. Would we approach life differently? Maybe we would have avoided certain unpleasant situations and events. If so, we would also have missed out on the experience from those situations, the lessons learned from our inappropriate decisions, and the pains life can bring.

We are who we are because of where we've been. This is neither good nor bad; it's just one of those things we can't change. We can learn from our experiences. In fact, we had better learn, or else we will keep committing the same errors in judgment time and again. Sometimes it seems we have to make the same mistakes over and over, but why that is, I don't know. Maybe the consequences weren't strong enough the first few times—the first hundred times, for that matter. Whatever the reason, at times it seems we have to repeat improper or damaging behavior before we can finally learn from our actions—before we can grow from our experiences. We just have to hit bottom, or at least get close enough to see the bottom, in order to decide to take action to fix things. As to what constitutes *bottom*, that's up to the individual. I've heard it said that we hit bottom when we stop digging. That makes sense to me. Finally, when we've had enough, we can begin to alter our behavior.

Regardless, whether we've had a good or a bad experience, the most important thing is what we take from our experiences. In my opinion, this is especially important with the not-so-pleasant ones. When we can learn from our past and become better individuals, then we can grow. If we take nothing from the past, then what have we accomplished? Just a good memory or a bad memory. For me, I would hope to develop knowledge that allows me to repeat the good experiences and shelve the bad experiences.

Life is really amazing. Sometimes it has a way of seeming so effortless, so easy, as though nothing can go wrong. Other times it's tougher than Chinese arithmetic, or Rubik's cube, or Chinese arithmetic multiplied by Rubik's cube. It can get pretty damned complicated. It's these difficult times that have the opportunity to present us with life's greatest lessons.

What can we do? What other course is there? There are no nonstop flights from who and where we were at birth to who and where we've become at present. We're a compilation of all the stops and experiences along the way, all the layovers and all the delays, the change of planes and the lost luggage, every one of the consequences of our actions and inactions. Maybe our experiences build character or make us stronger; maybe we withdraw or become weaker. Whatever the case, they most certainly affect us—most likely not neutrally.

When a waiter brings us a hot plate, saying, "Watch out, *hot plate*!" what do we almost always instinctively do? We touch the plate to see how hot it is; we have to find out for ourselves. Hopefully we have learned not to grab it with both hands, or to stick our tongues on it, but we have to test it nonetheless. Such is the case with many situations in life.

Then there are the bigger, more serious things we may have struggled with in life, like jail, drug abuse, alcoholism, gambling, or overspending. At one point we thought such things as, I probably shouldn't have driven while drunk, or robbed that store, or hit that guy, and then I wouldn't be in jail. Well, we did it. It's over; it's in the past. All that can be done is to pay the consequences and hopefully learn from the experience, and then move on. A lot of times, committing the action is easy; owning up to it is the hard part. We all make mistakes. It's what we do with them that will determine what kind of person we will be.

We are works in progress. What we do today will shape who we are tomorrow. Therefore, we mustn't run or try to hide from what we've done in the past. First of all, we can't change it; it's done. It's history. The best we can do is try to learn from our experiences. Then and only then may it be possible to put them to rest. Embrace them, regardless of how distasteful that thought may be, and then move on. Our past is all part of our present. If we try to do the best we possibly can, it will lead us to a better, more positive tomorrow. Alternatively, if we try to ignore the unpleasant experiences, if we fail to face them, we may miss the opportunity to learn from them and grow from them.

I wrote the above piece, "Personal Itinerary," after a phone conversation with my mom. I hadn't been in recovery for very long, but I was making good progress. I was implementing many changes in myself and in my life. This evolution is ongoing, and if I do things right it will never end. There were a lot of outward changes in me, ones obvious to my family and close friends. My mom kept going on about how great I was doing and how happy she was for me. She was also exhibiting a case of the *but ifs*—but if this hadn't happened, but if you hadn't have done that, everything would be great. She couldn't see what was plainly obvious to me. The simple fact of the matter was that if I hadn't gotten myself into the situations I had, if I hadn't put myself through the pain and suffering I endured, I would never have found the path I'm currently on. It goes back to the *hitting bottom* referenced above. Until I got to the point where I couldn't endure anymore, it was impossible for me to take the action necessary to get my life to where it is now.

That's when it hit me. No matter how similar our situation may be to someone else's, we've all taken different paths to get where we now are. Our journeys are all unique. Some of us may end up in the same place, but we've almost certainly taken different routes. Our journeys may be like others, but they are nonetheless specific to us. They are ours and ours alone. We are experts on our own experiences. No one else knows them as intimately as we ourselves do. All this being said, what do we do when we finally realize it's time for a change?

Just like the paths into our current situations, the ones leading out will probably be unique. Therefore, I can only tell you what has worked for me. I can only express my opinions and my observations. How you choose to interpret them, and whether you decide to implement any of these tools is completely up to you. All I can tell you is what has seemed to work for me.

I never planned on changing my whole life. My original goal was to merely remove certain destructive behaviors from my daily routine. I thought I was just going to address a few negative habits I had acquired early in life, ones that over the years had grown into all-consuming beasts. I really had no idea what I was getting into. I had no idea how I was going to go about making the changes I was keen on making. All I know for sure is that the desire for change was there.

In hindsight, I can see that my motives weren't pure. What I mean by that is that part of my motivation was geared toward making changes for someone other than me. At the time it seemed insignificant, but I've since realized that unless I was willing to make these changes solely for myself, my chances for success would be greatly diminished. Don't get me wrong; when you're dealing with alcoholism or a substance-abuse problem, the important thing is to take that first step.

For me, my wife was a big motivator. She had decided to go into treatment, prior to my decision to take another shot at sobriety. We both had already made a couple of attempts at getting clean over the previous year. This time, she had chosen a facility in the Los Angeles area, far from our hometown of Columbus, Ohio. I'm pretty confident that if we had failed this time, we would have lost everything: children, family, job, house, and each other.

Even with all that at stake, I had a difficult time figuring out what to do first. My mind and decision-making process were so distorted by my increased ability to rationalize and my huge capacity for denial that it was difficult to make the right decision or even know what the right decision was. Even after my wife went into rehab, and I decided to get clean, I continued to nurse the notion that I would be able to limit my substance use to special occasions. Of course, I had to keep this thought secret, because I didn't want to have a negative effect on my wife's recovery. After all, she was the one with the problem; I could control things. As ridiculous as this sounds now, at the time I really believed it.

That was a big problem at first: comparing myself and my addiction to others and their problems and behavior. By letting my mind call the shots, I was able to rationalize my continued use and deny the fact that my life had become completely unmanageable. As I look back now, I can see that as things got worse, I merely changed my definition of manageability. I lowered its requirements. There's nothing shocking about this, at least not to those around me, and in reality, not even to myself. Although it's easier to see now, even then I knew in the back of my mind that things had to change. The problem was that up to that point, I still wasn't ready to make that change. I didn't want to lose my wife and kids. They were all I had left. I'd spent everything, and gone into debt. I still had some resources, but they weren't going to last much longer. I was either going to end up in jail or die all alone.

Honesty

George Washington, our first president and one of our country's founding fathers, once said, or so it's been told, "I cannot tell a lie." I'm sorry, but I think he was lying when he said that. Of course he could tell a lie; he was a human being. Hell, he was a general in our armed forces. He was a politician. He had to have lied at one time or another. Maybe they were just little ones, white lies and half-truths, whatever. We have all at one time or another told a lie or at least pleaded the Fifth.

On this topic I may be safe in breaking my own personal rule on the absolutes *always* and *never*. I'm going out on a limb here and stating in print that there's no one, no mere mortal, who has always told the truth and never told a lie, at least a little one. I will, however, qualify that the lie need not necessarily be to another human being. It could be to a pet; you know, you're going on a trip, the dog sees the suitcases and gets sad, so you say, "Don't worry, Rover, I won't be gone long." Now, you may be going to Europe for six months, but still you tell Rover, "I'll be right back."

Lastly, in the event that you have never even lied to your pet, what about yourself? Have you ever lied to yourself? Somewhere along the way, I'm sure you must have been dishonest with yourself. No, these pants don't make me look fat. I'm not drunk; I can drive. At one time or another, you have not been completely honest with yourself. I know this was the case with me, way too many times to even attempt to count.

I think most people try to be honest, at least as far as the big things go. Those little things, though, they can be a bitch. A lot of times it's easy to tell yourself—or at least I do—that it's okay because I'm lying to spare someone's feelings or to avoid upsetting them. Then there are the times when, for whatever reason, I just don't want to pay the price that complete honesty will extract from me. A lot of times, the lie was something petty or senseless. Nonetheless, on many occasions I have found myself too selfish or frightened to tell the absolute truth. It's a habit I'm really trying to change.

As I work on this character defect, I've made some interesting discoveries. For me, the most important thing is to try and be completely honest with myself. When I am able to do this— which I'm happy to say is most of the time these days—it makes being honest about the big things much easier. I am an alcoholic and an addict, a combination that makes it virtually impossible to tell the truth, at least when I was using—well, *especially* when I was using. I'm fundamentally a good person. It's just that the lifestyle I was leading created a wealth of situations in which I felt I had no option but to lie. The small lies were too numerous to tally, and the big ones, while not as frequent, numbered enough to keep them off the endangered species list. Since I've been in recovery, trying to apply a new set of principles to my life, the truth has not only been much easier to find, it has also been a lot easier to disseminate. I'm not saying that it's always easy. It's just a lot more palatable these days. When I'm honest, I feel much better about myself, maybe not right at the crucial moment of confession, but if not then, fairly soon thereafter.

When I concentrate on the little things, ones I wouldn't have given a thought to in the past, not only do I encounter the bigger problem areas far less frequently, but when I do find myself in a morally painful quarter, things are much easier to deal with. This may sound simplistic, but for me it was far from easy for quite some time. Since I have been trying to do the right thing I can honestly say that I haven't been faced with any huge dilemmas as far as the truth goes. I'm avoiding decisions and actions that in the past would propel me to a point where I would feel it necessary to lie.

I was less than thirty days sober when I wrote the above thoughts on honesty. I had always been brought up to tell the truth. For the most part, I did. There were times when I didn't, in certain instances when I felt the pain associated with complete honesty would have been too much to handle. Then there were the times when I was just trying to spare someone's feelings. In retrospect, those occasions were the easy ones to pick out. The ability to be honest with myself is a little more difficult to pin down. I would like to think that I usually was, but I can't make that statement with any certainty. The fact that I started to use alcohol and drugs at such a young age makes it difficult for me to truly determine what level of honesty I practiced with myself growing up.

The important thing is that I am finally capable of being honest with myself. Practicing such self-honesty is by no means a 100 percent done deal. I still have to work on it. I still have to grow as a person. There are still situations in which I may think I'm being honest with myself, but in reality I am not. My alcoholic/addict mind is always capable of trying to convince me of something that isn't the truth. As I continue to work on myself, it is becoming easier to spot such situations.

My decision to get clean was precipitated by a combination of factors. Self-honesty was one of them, and the desire to make changes in my life was another. I think timing also played a big part. By timing I simply mean that things happen when they're supposed to happen, when the time is right. Not everyone will agree with this. For me, though, I don't think I would have had the desire unless I had reached the point where it was time for a change. I've heard stories about a moment of clarity, a flash of light, a voice from above. I can tell you that none of that happened to me. My experience was more a whimper from the deep recesses of my mind, maybe my subconscious, something saying, "You have to do something. You can't keep living like this." I had no idea what I was going to do. I wasn't even completely sure why I was going to do it. I just knew I had to do something.

As I mentioned earlier, my wife had recently left for a rehab stint in California. I had already done a thirty-day program the previous year and had no intention of going back to another such place. I was firmly of the mindset that I failed in my earlier attempts at sobriety because I hadn't been ready to quit yet. What could they tell me at another rehab facility that they hadn't told me last year? Drugs are bad! Don't do them! I was convinced I could do it on my own.

Now, I can look back at things and laugh. I was really confused. I was going to get clean and sober, because things were different this time. I was ready. I had the desire. I should add that my goal was to stop using cocaine, except for special occasions. At the time I thought I would still be able to drink moderately, smoke some weed, and possibly dabble in a few other substances. As I said, I was really confused. The important thing was that I was going to do something, and I truly was more motivated this time around. The negative consequences of my behavior were becoming more frequent and more serious—much more serious.

For this, my third real attempt at getting clean, I had decided to leave the country, to go to Europe. My thoughts were that I needed to be someplace where I could get over the hump. Europe seemed perfect. After all, it was where I had gone the second time I tried to quit. The important thing for me was to get away from my current surroundings, the people and places associated with my everyday drug use. I wanted to be alone. I wanted to have time to write and reflect on my past and my current situation. I also love to travel and explore new places. I thought that keeping myself occupied would ease my transition from complete dependence on cocaine to a daily routine without it. Upon my return to the States, I promised my wife that I would enroll in an intensive outpatient program at a local rehab center.

At this point I have to say that I didn't believe, truly believe, that any additional drug rehabilitation education was going to make much of a difference in my situation. I was still of the opinion that if you wanted to quit, you could quit. In the beginning of my attempt to quit, I had no idea what was involved in a twelve-step program. I didn't know that there is a difference between abstinence and sobriety. In the beginning, the keys for me were a newfound honesty with myself and open-mindedness. However, there was definitely a lag between the open-mindedness and the honesty. The honesty led me to the realization that I didn't know everything and that my decision-making process was severely flawed. I did, however, have a toehold that helped me take the first steps of an incredible journey.

My first week in Europe was truly difficult. As a chemical dependent, I was full of fear, among other things, the actual physical act of stopping being right at the top of the list. Any alcoholic or addict will know what I'm talking about. It's almost inconceivable to imagine that last hit or that last drink. The will to stop, the desire to quit, isn't enough by itself, at least not for me. I knew I had to stop. I had a plan, but being the good addict that I am, I had convinced myself that the best course of action would be to make sure I had enough drugs to get me through the first few days of my trip. I was scared to death to continue the way I was going, but I was even more afraid of quitting.

There's no real logic in my decision to smuggle drugs into a foreign country. It's just another example of my addict mentality. Over the previous thirty years, I had traveled to Europe at least fifteen times, but except for my previous attempt to get clean three months earlier, I really can't remember trying to bring any drugs with me. Even before 9/11, I was sane enough to realize the hazards of traveling overseas with a controlled substance. Post 9/11, such behavior was simply insane. It's tough enough to get a lighter through security, let alone drugs and paraphernalia. Nonetheless, I was to the point that such risky behavior made sense. Furthermore, I was so out of control that not only did I have to take the drugs with me, I had to bring them in my carry-on, so I could get high at the airports and on the planes. Keep in mind that I wasn't sneaking lines; I was smoking. It's very difficult to be inconspicuous with a pipe and a lighter, especially in an airport or on an airplane. Somehow I made it.

My original plan called for settling down in Amsterdam for a few days. Actually, it was three. I stretched it out to four. Seriously, as I look back on it, only an addict would choose to go to Amsterdam to quit doing drugs. My rationale at the time was that there I could get some good hash in order to ease the anxiety of quitting. In reality, sticking around in Amsterdam was just an excuse to stay high for a few more days, but that was okay because I was going to do something about my addiction. I was going to quit. I really started to panic after a few days in the city. I was running low. What was I going to do? I wanted to quit, but just not right then. I was able to find a connection and secure enough stuff to keep me good and high for three or four more days. That's when I made my first good decision of the trip.

I booked a night train to Munich on the fourth day. I knew I had to go someplace where it would be virtually impossible to find any more drugs. I spent three days and nights in Munich, mostly in my hotel room, contemplating what lay ahead of me. It was a very difficult time, much tougher than my previous attempts at sobriety. I was alone. My wife was in rehab seven thousand miles away. There was really no one for me to call or talk to. For that matter, there was really no one I wanted to talk to. As my supplies dwindled, I grew more agitated and aggravated. I was angry. I was also full of resentment—resentment toward everyone.

For the most part, my journaling was illegible and irrational. The thoughts I was putting down on paper reflected the turmoil going on inside me. As I began to examine my life and the situation I was in, I started to realize some of what I had put my family through. It was the start of the process of owning up to some of my deficiencies as a father, a husband, a son, and a person.

Obligations

What a scary word, at least for me. I'm trying to decide if it is more worrisome now or when I was using. I used to tell myself when I was using or drinking that I wasn't hurting anybody else, it was my life, and I could do with it as I pleased. I was wrong.

When I was in Europe, I began to think about my obligations and duties to my family and my fellow man. There are different types of obligations. There are obligations to others, things I must do either because I have made a promise or because they are necessitated by my circumstances.

I am a father. I have a duty to take care of my children, not because I have promised them, but because I inherently owe them certain things. I have responsibilities to my fellow man, simply because I inhabit this planet. I have obligations to myself, because if I'm not true to myself I will surely become difficult to live with. I will have an arduous existence if I can't look in the mirror every day and honestly say, hey, you're doing a pretty good job; keep it up.

I know that for me there was a time when I didn't pay much attention to these various types of obligations. Sure, I knew I had to pay my bills, but I did so either when it was convenient for me or when someone was going to do something to me or take something from me because of my procrastination. When I was heavily into my addiction, it didn't even bother me that I was about to face some sort of negative consequences for not owning up to my obligations. So long as I could somehow, some way, slide by with minimal pain, I was willing to let things go as long as possible.

I shirked obligations to my family. I made sure my kids had a roof over their heads and food to eat. But I was very lax in other areas, mostly with my time and the quality of the time that I did manage to give them. I was too self-centered to give all that I could give, or to be all that I could be to them. I'm not sure which was worse, my failure to adequately take care of these obligations, or the fact that I convinced myself that I was doing a pretty good job, that there were a lot of parents who were doing less than I was. Whether or not this was true, I was not living up to my responsibilities and obligations.

I can see it now. I am changing it now. I must always be cognizant of the fact that it is very easy to get complacent, to get a little selfish when it comes to the needs of others.

I have obligations to others because I have made promises or committed myself to take on certain tasks. These commitments are easy to slip on, especially the ones I am doing as a favor, the ones only my promise requires me to act on. I used to think, well, I'll get the task done eventually, and I usually did. Now I realize I need to act on such commitments quickly, because although they may not be a big deal to me, they may very well be a big deal to the person I've made a promise to. The commitment may be writing a letter for someone, running an errand, or doing a chore. It really doesn't matter what the task is. If I can act on it in a timely manner, especially if I have indicated that the job will be done by a certain time, I will be fulfilling two obligations: one to the person I have promised, and one to me. When I say I'm going to do something, I own it. That responsibility is mine. If I fail, I fail not only the person I promised, but also myself.

Many times, the negative repercussions of failure to act might be greater to me. The promise might be as simple as picking up a gallon of milk for someone. If I don't do it, for whatever reason, the person may be quite capable of performing the task for himself. He may be no more than slightly inconvenienced by my failure, but I will have to live with my inability to deliver on an obligation that I accepted. Failing at even something as simple as a promise to go to the store is something I have to live with, something that impacts me as a person.

What good is my word if I can't deliver on the small things? Can I trust myself with the larger tasks in life? Maybe I will deliver on the big ones; maybe I won't. For me, it's more a matter of how I want to live my life. I want people to be able to count on me.

Being on time is another good example. If I promise to be somewhere or to do something at a certain time and then show up late or not at all, I may cause more problems than if I had never made the promise at all. At least if I hadn't committed myself, the person counting on me could have made other arrangements. In the past I might have said, "Oh well, I was trying to do you a favor; sorry I'm late." Sure, things happen that cause us to be unable to deliver on obligations in life. I just want to try and make sure that I am not that thing.

I would like to say that all these realizations just came rushing in on me while I was sitting in my hotel room in Munich, but that's not the case. I was just beginning to get honest with myself, assessing my life and the areas where I had been remiss. I started to focus on my family and the problems I had caused as a result of my addiction. This was a very difficult time for me. Even though I realized that denying my circumstances was no longer an option, I was only just scratching the surface. Introspection revealed many layers of rationalization of past behavior and events. At the time, I had no idea how deep I was going to have to dig in order to uncover all past acts I would have to rectify. Furthermore, I was uncertain whether or not all of them could be remedied.

I think part of my despair was due to the fact that although I knew I was broken, I still had no idea how I was going to fix myself. Sure, I knew I had to change. I had a sincere desire to change. I just wasn't sure how to go about it. The only solution my mind was able to come up with was to give up cocaine. Okay. No problem, I thought, I'll just quit when I finish what's left of my stash. I probably had less than a day's supply left.

I can still remember my last hit, vividly. It was a Friday afternoon, a little bit after the lunch hour. Normal peoples' lunch hour, not mine; I hadn't eaten much the past few days. I hadn't eaten much the past year. That's what I would do. I would go walk around Munich, eat lunch, and see the sights—after I enjoyed my last hit, of course. I was going to savor it for all it was worth. After all, that was it; I was through. No more! But a minute or two after exhaling that last hit, I wanted more. I can remember searching the carpet, furniture, any place a rock might have dropped. No luck. That was okay; it was time to get out of the hotel room. It was time to start getting clean. Wait, I thought, there might be some resin in a few of my pipes. There was. I smoked them clean, until not a trace was left.

Up to that point, I really hadn't taken any action. I talked about quitting. I made plans about how I could go about quitting. I had even started to write down some of the damaging things I had done to others and myself and what I was going to do to make things better. The one thing I hadn't done yet was actually quit. I used to think that all I did was procrastinate and waste time my first week in Europe, but I don't necessarily feel that way anymore. Everyone's journey is different. I believe everything happens when it's supposed to happen.

For me, my last week of use was filled with many different emotions. To this day, I think of how I felt at certain times that first week, and it helps me to get through difficult times, to deal with cravings and temptation. It's all part of my past, all part of my journey to where I am today. At the time, I had no idea what was ahead of me. I knew that I was broken. I just had to figure out how I was going to get fixed.

That's when I made my second good decision. Munich had served its purpose. It was time to move on. I decided to go east, away from Amsterdam, farther away from the States. I went to the station and bought a ticket for an afternoon train. I was going to Salzburg, Austria. I began my transition from active addict to recovering addict on that train trip from Germany to Austria. I had a lot of problems and questions, but no solutions. What I did have was a little over twenty-four hours with no cocaine. I also had fear, anger, resentment, and guilt, among other things. That was enough to start with. The important thing, the really amazing thing to me, was that I had made a start.

One of the missions of rehabilitation, which I'd learned about at my first treatment center, involved rewiring the addict's brain. Apparently, we have a tendency to glorify our drinking and drugging. Our brains have a way of preparing memory files that store the good times related to our use and omit many of the negative consequences involved. The depressing recollections are stored somewhere; we just don't think about them as often. I would imagine it has something to do with our denial and rationalization defenses.

Rewriting, or restamping, a file with an honest and factual account of what actually happened is part of the process of recovery. Some of this began happening naturally for me as I slipped closer to my bottom. It became more and more difficult to deny the fact that alcohol and/or drugs had usually, if not always, played some part in the negative events of my life.

I decided to take this rewiring exercise a step further in my current recovery plan. By choice, I had left on this trip to Europe without a camera. The only recording I planned to do was in my journals. Now that I was relieved of the preoccupation of getting high, I could concentrate on getting out and exploring new places. I started seeing amazing sights, wonderful images of new places everywhere I turned. I toyed with the idea of getting a camera, even a disposable one, so I would have some images to look back on at the end of my trip. Instead, I decided to keep these new files that I was creating completely internal, for my mind only. I mentally labeled all the new, wonderful images with this tag: Europe, March, 2007. Then I imprinted the reason why I was here on each one as they were formed: *You are here because without change you will lose everything in your life that is important: your wife and kids, a life that has so much to offer.* My hope is that when I think of these images, I will see this warning sign on each and every one of them.

It was very important that I stay busy. I needed to keep my mind occupied so I wouldn't start thinking about not being high. After all, distracting myself by exploring new places was one of the reasons for coming to Europe. There was so much to see here, so much to explore. One of my hobbies prior to becoming a full-time drug abuser was history. I am particularly enthralled with both of the World Wars. On the way to Salzburg, I noticed that Berchtesgaden, Germany, was only about an hour's train ride away. My goal was to get some rest and do some exploring the following day. I didn't realize it at the time, but tomorrow was going to be a big day.

I awoke this particular day with mixed feelings. Part of me wanted to get going, to do something. The other part was emotionally, mentally, and physically drained. It would have been very easy to stay in bed all day. I can still remember my last hit, that last huge release of dopamine. How was I going to get that feeling again? Anyone who's ever used alcohol or drugs to achieve that euphoric feeling, and instant gratification, will know what I'm talking about. I had been using chemicals to buoy myself for well over a year, pretty much 24/7, except for when I slept, which was infrequently. I had lost track of what it felt like to feel normal.

I vacillated back and forth about whether I should attempt to go to Berchtesgaden. At the time, it sure seemed like a lot of work. For whatever reason, I made the decision to go. It was a ten- or fifteen-minute cab ride to the train station, or about a forty-five-minute walk. Don't ask me why, but I decided to walk. Shortly after departing the hotel, I had a wonderful feeling. At first I felt confused, because it almost felt as though I'd just done a big hit. Then I realized that I must be releasing neurotransmitters—dopamine, endorphins—the old-fashioned way. I was exploring. I was doing something that I loved to do. It was a truly amazing feeling. I had forgotten that I could get this feeling without using chemicals. It seems silly now, but I had become completely reliant on getting what I wanted, when I wanted it, by using drugs. I think I had come to believe that there was no other way.

This event was important to me in two ways. It not only reminded me that I was capable of achieving a natural high and enjoying life without the use of chemicals, but it also freed up my mind, which enabled me to begin to examine my other problems, the ones that fueled my addiction.

At the time, I had no idea of the number of changes I would soon be making in my life, not only in the way I lived it, but in the manner I looked at it and approached it as well. About five or six weeks later, a counselor would sum things up quite well during one of my group sessions. He told all of us there, "An addict only has to change one thing: everything." Not only did I not know what I would have to change, I still had no idea where to start. I was beginning to pat myself on the back for abstaining from cocaine for a little over two days. Other than beginning to get honest with myself, I really hadn't accomplished much, except, as I would learn later, realizing that a little honesty can go a long way, especially when you're being honest with yourself.

Honesty is the key for me. Honesty cracks the door for open-mindedness, without which I have no chance at change. Through honesty, I am able to address my flaws and character defects, of which there are many. I am better able to observe and assess life and its many mysteries.

One thing that struck me after a few days without my drug of choice was the absence of the extreme feelings of anxiety and despair that had enveloped me in the past whenever I was without my cocaine. When I was using, time usually seemed to fly by. When I was without it, minutes seemed like hours, and hours passed like days. There was nothing worse than having to wait a day or two to get resupplied. I had devoted most of my energy and resources to making sure that I never ran out. Those dry times were sheer misery. Why the perceived disparity in the passage of time?

Time Passage

I have a few observations on time, or more precisely the passage of it, that I'd like to share. As we're all aware, time can pass slowly or it can pass quickly. We've all experienced this firsthand. Have you ever really examined this issue in your life?

Sixty seconds in a minute, sixty minutes in an hour, twenty-four hours in a day. A minute's a minute, sixty ticks of the second hand ... whether you're happy, sad, angry, anxious, depressed, excited ... with new friends, with old friends, with strangers, or by yourself. It doesn't matter. It could be sunny; it could be raining. Maybe it's a hot day; maybe it's cold. Monday or Saturday, daytime or nighttime, it just doesn't matter. Whatever your mood, wherever you are, whatever the weather, sixty seconds is sixty seconds, is a minute, one-sixtieth of an hour.

Why, then, is there such a disparity in our sense of how fast (or how slow) time goes by? It can fly by. It can crawl. It can change our attitudes, our demeanor, and the way we interact with others, the way we feel about ourselves.

Initially, we all probably shrug such thinking off. Hey, time flies when you're occupied, when you're doing something you enjoy, when you're having fun. On the other hand, it passes slowly if you're not happy with the place you are occupying at any given moment or with something around you—a person or thing, or even yourself. Maybe it's the activity in which you are involved at that moment—or the lack of activity.

Yes. True. I understand all of that, but how can it seem so completely, utterly different in its perceived rate of passage? Sixty seconds is sixty seconds is sixty seconds. How can eight hours seem like one hour when I'm at Disneyland? How can four hours seem like an entire day when I'm strapped into an airplane seat? Time seems to run slower, agonizingly slow in some situations.

It's probably good that we perceive time's passage at different rates. Life goes by fast enough as it is. Just ask me—or better yet, ask anyone who is forty, fifty, sixty, seventy, eighty years old. The present and the future have a knack of becoming the past in what appears to be the blink of an eye, even with the bad times dragging on at what appears to be a snail's pace. Even with these disparities, time is ahead of us, then we're in the moment, and then whoosh. It's gone, vanished. It's history. Moments, minutes, hours, years— never to be in the future or even the present again.

The best we can do is to relive these moments in our minds, in our hearts, and in our souls. We can rerun them again and again, over and over, but all we're really doing is utilizing what precious time we have left on moments and events that are behind us forever. Indeed, time waits for no one. It marches forward without cessation, without pause, without a care as to how we are feeling or how we're doing at any given moment. It may pass quickly, it may drag on slowly, but it is advancing each moment, every second unique and specific, never to be seen or heard from again. We should all do our best to enjoy each fleeting moment. We can relive the good times in our dreams, or pay them brief homage while we are conscious. But let's not dwell on the past, even past good times, because we may miss out on something that's just as good, maybe even better. And as for dwelling on the bad times … *what a waste of time.*

I was making good use of my time in Europe. My days and evenings were full. I wrote, I read, I walked and explored. I really began to get a handle on where I was in life. I definitely had a bit of anxiety about going Stateside. I've always been very comfortable about traveling abroad alone. For me, it offers a perfect environment for self reflection. If I choose to do so, I can isolate, even in a city of millions. I can also interact with the citizens of the locales I'm visiting. As a rule of thumb, I tend to shy away from the tourists, especially Americans. I can intermingle with them when I'm at home.

I was afraid to go home. I even canceled my return flight. I felt safe where I was, distanced from my past and removed from the future that awaited my return. As long as I stayed in Europe, I had to deal only with myself. I could postpone repairing my relationships with family and friends. For how long, I didn't know. I just knew that I wasn't ready yet.

When I look back now, I can see that I was no different from most addicts who have spent any length of time in a treatment center. The prospect of transitioning back into the real world from a safe environment can be very troubling. In fact, it is a trait my wife would exhibit several weeks later, one I would become highly critical of. I can now see that I was no different from her in this respect. The only difference was that her safe haven was a typical treatment center; mine was a continent.

There were many who balked at my initial plan of recovery: travel to Europe for a few weeks and get clean, then attend a local intensive outpatient program of recovery. At the time, I had no idea what an IOP even consisted of. I figured it was like some sort of night school for alcoholics and addicts. Beyond that, I was clueless about what such a program would entail. Although part of me was still interested in seeking additional help, another part was of the notion that merely giving up cocaine, or at least drastically reducing my consumption—controlling my intake so to speak— would be enough to get my life on the right track. Although I had gained some insight into sanity, I was still emotionally and spiritually lost. I had a vague idea of where I wanted to go but no idea about how I was going to get there.

I had originally scheduled my trip to roughly coincide with my wife's release from her treatment center. Around this time, I learned that she intended to stay for an additional three weeks. I just couldn't understand why someone would want to do that. I had already been to a conventional rehab facility. What could they tell you or teach you in seven weeks that they couldn't accomplish in four? I was very skeptical of these programs because of the amount of money they charged for doing basically what I was doing by myself, or least that's how I thought about it at the time. I was wrong. Looking back, I can see that I was 100 percent, emphatically wrong. It's tough enough to get the upper hand on addiction, any addiction. Addicts need to avail ourselves of all the help, strength, and support, all of the resources available to us when we make the decision to take on such a formidable opponent as drugs and alcohol. Although there may not be an easy way out, some ways are harder than others.

I was beginning to develop some rather large resentments during this portion of my recovery, or what I thought was my recovery. I really should call it my initial period of cocaine abstinence, because after all, I was still drinking, smoking a little hash, and taking the occasional Valium in order to calm down. There was also the intermittent use of pain pills; of course, these were for medicinal purposes only, since I took them only when something hurt. I didn't take the pain pills very often anymore, because, well, they were almost gone. In my mind, I thought I was doing a pretty good job. I thought I was coming to terms with my problems. In reality, I was just beginning to realize what the problems were. I had to start somewhere, however, and now that I had, the important thing was to keep moving in the right direction.

I loved my wife. I missed my wife. Other than one or two phone conversations with our nanny, who was watching over our young son, my wife was the only other person I spoke with during my trip. All the credit for my current foray into sobriety belongs to her. We had talked about it on countless occasions. The conversation usually went something like this: "We have to do something. We can't keep living like this." Although the frequency of these conversations increased, we never seemed to be able to take any action. On the rare occasions when we did, it was usually no more than a dressed-up attempt at controlling our use.

While I was mentally wrestling with varying plans tailored to moderate my addiction, my wife had come to the conclusion that, at least for her, rehab was the only way out. Like it or not, if she was going to try and do something about it, I had to do something as well. That was my impetus for my current stab at sobriety. We wanted to stick together. We had ridden the elevator down as a team, and we wanted to get out of the hole we had dug, together. With one exception, however: I wasn't going to any rehab facility. I was going to prepare my own curriculum of recovery. Our thoughts were that it didn't matter how we did it, just so we did it and ended up in the same place.

Great! You do it your way, and I'll do it my way, and we'll meet at the corner of Recovery and Serenity in about a month. Things didn't go that smoothly. I can only speak for myself, but I was really messed up. To compound matters even more, my communication and relationship skills had fallen to an all-time low. I guess drug addiction has a tendency to reduce one's people skills. At least it did in my case. Furthermore, my custom-designed recovery plan was delayed by an emergency appendectomy. The bottom line was that my wife had already been in rehab for about a month when I was doing my last hit. Needless to say, I was little bit behind the curve.

Although we were trying to do the same thing, we were going about it in completely different ways. I think it is imperative that people enter into a program of recovery solely for their own well-being. In my situation, I viewed rehabilitation as a necessity in order to save my wife and family. This presented problems for me, especially with my wife. The resentment and anger I was harboring from past acts began to grow, because I didn't feel I was getting enough credit for my actions on certain occasions. Whether this is actually true, I don't know. The point is that as long as I felt, even in the smallest way, that I was getting clean for someone else, and not completely for myself and my own well-being, resentment was sure to follow.

It was around this time that I received some advice from one of the therapists at my wife's treatment center. This particular conversation took place a couple of days after a ninety-minute conjoint telephone conference in which I pretty much did all the talking. To describe my monologue on that occasion as *talking* would be a slight understatement. Suffice it to say I was very agitated during this conference. The therapist's advice that followed was a simple suggestion, one I'd heard before, advice that I had probably given before. It was also counsel that I don't believe I ever really paid much attention to: *Let go of the past*. It was my decision. In this particular instance, it was up to me. If I wanted to save my marriage and move forward, I had to come to terms with the past.

Did I want to save my marriage? That straightforward yes-or-no question put things in a very simple context for me. It was the first time that it was suggested to me that much of my anger and resentment was leftover baggage from events gone by, and it is a great example of another baby step in my recovery process. Of course I wanted to save my marriage. I loved my wife—my wife and kids—more than anything on this earth.

Shortly after this conversation, I made a conscious effort to put certain things behind me and rededicate myself to my wife and our marriage. In the weeks and months to come I would learn to apply this simple nugget of wisdom, letting go of the past, to other segments of my personal history, thus eradicating many demons.

Avoiding resentment and anger is one of the cornerstones of my newfound sobriety. I understand that it is unrealistic to think that I will never cross paths with these destructive human emotions again. After all, I am human. I am, however, practicing a new way of life in which their occurrences are less frequent, and when they do occur, they are much shorter and less intense.

Resentment

This is not only a tremendously important subject, a subject we have all confronted at some point in our lives, but most of us are probably still dealing with it to some degree.

Most have some person, place, thing, or situation about which we continue to harbor some resentment. Maybe it's not a blinding resentment, one that impairs our ability to see and think clearly and honestly. It might be no more than a minor nuisance, something like, "I'm never going back to that place, I had bad service; the weather was horrible; or I got in an accident going that way." Whatever the cause is just doesn't matter. Resentment is such an atrocious and sometimes all-consuming emotion. It is one that can literally take a life, usually that of the holder of the resentment. To a lesser degree, resentment can make life miserable, even if the bearer doesn't realize it at the time. It can steal precious moments, right in front of us, in our present. Precious periods of time—time which is too short as it is—only because we're angry about the past. It doesn't matter whether the cause is a person, place, or thing; animal, vegetable, or mineral; real or imagined.

Resentment is in effect shortening our lives, because we are not living them to their fullest potential. We're not living, enjoying the present, and all because of something that may be long gone. Something we can't change now, probably couldn't change then, and most likely won't be able to change if it happens again in the future. We can only control ourselves—maybe.

Why don't we resent ourselves when we do things we're not pleased with? No, resentment is too tough. When we ourselves perpetrate something unsavory, we have a gentler feeling: regret. Maybe it's because we can't shut ourselves off from ourselves. We still have to live with ourselves, so we regret instead of resent.

I'm completely serious. This correlation just hit me as I was writing it. It's never even entered my mind to compare and contrast resentment and regret. I imagine I'll end up spending quite a bit of time examining their relationship to each other.

This is such a serious topic. I have shut people out my life because of resentment—close people, family members. In fact, it has usually been the people who are closest to me whom I choose to shun the most severely, the ones on whom I have imposed the death sentence. By eliminating all contact it was easier for me to convince myself that my resentment was justified, that I had a right to be angry and to lay the blame on someone else.

I'm trying to think of the last stranger I've resented. I can't think of any, because for the most part, they don't affect my life.

For me, as I reflect, and if I'm truly honest with myself, most of, if not all of the really bad situations I've encountered … the ones where the most severe cases of resentment have emanated from … well, when I really get to the heart of the matter, I tend to bump into an old familiar face. MINE! Few and far between, if at all, are the times when someone has decided to intrude on my life and disrupt my happy feelings with misery, pain, and suffering, if I haven't somehow in some way played a part in the matter.

The more I grow and the more I learn, the more important it is for me to do my best to keep anger and resentment at bay. I still have to just let things out sometimes. I think that we all do. It's only natural. One thing that helps me when I feel my temperature starting to rise is to pause before I react. This simple act not only has the effect of tempering my initial response, but it also affords me an opportunity to examine the root of my discontent.

To pause, to have that ability to delay, even for the briefest of moments, my inevitable feelings or response to a given situation is also the first step in another even more important tool that I am beginning to implement in my daily life. Patience. Patience, tolerance, acceptance, and the ability to relinquish control are principles and practices I would be exposed to shortly after I returned from Europe. Although these are values I believe I have possessed to some extent for quite some time, my implementation of them could be quite selective at best, and at times almost nonexistent. It was important for me to realize that whenever I react to something immediately, I have forgone the opportunity to be patient. I may be able to recant, but I can't change what I've already said or done. The cat is already out of the bag, and whether or not it can be put back is another question.

I had acquired a few pieces to the puzzle. As of yet I still didn't know how they would fit together or what the picture would look like. I was, however, becoming curious. I was starting to peek out of the box which I had put myself in. I was beginning to wonder what life was really all about. This wasn't a new thought for me. It was more of a forgotten one. In some respects I had really simplified life for the past year and a half: get drugs, get high, get more drugs, and repeat. This simplification process had a very high price. I had gotten to the point where the only certainties in my life were that I had: *Uncertainty in Myself, Uncertainty in My Wife, and Uncertainty in My Life.*

I wanted some certainty back in my life. It was time to start thinking about going home. My younger daughter's birthday was coming up in a few days. I would try to be there for it. My mom was also in town visiting my kids. I had spoken with her a few days earlier and told her I didn't think I was ready to come home, that I needed more time abroad to sort things out. She was on board with whatever I needed to do in order to get clean.

I was able to book a Friday flight home, and my daughter's birthday was Sunday. This would give me a day to rest and regroup. The majority of my drug abuse had taken place in my bedroom. It had been a sanctuary for the past almost year and a half. In a sense, going home was also going to be like returning to a crime scene. Even though I had gotten rid of most of my paraphernalia before departing for Europe, there were sure to be some remnants of my past scattered here and there. I would just have to deal with that when the time came.

I could plan all I wanted to. The fact of the matter was, I had no idea how I was going to react to certain situations until I was smack dab in the middle of them. To this point, I still hadn't acquired the necessary tools or the necessary support group, which I now believe is crucial for a successful recovery. Up to now, all I had really been doing was latching onto whatever idea or thought I came across that afforded me some sort of hope or optimism.

My wife, my kids—I didn't want to lose them. I was beginning to think seriously about consequences. When I was lost in the middle of my addiction, consequences were the furthest thing from my mind. I knew they were out there somewhere, but they just seemed insignificant compared to the act of staying high. This may be one of the most difficult concepts for nonaddicts to understand. I can empathize. I was there, and it's still hard for me to understand some of the things I did. I am convinced that our brains truly lose the ability to function rationally.

It was around this time, while I was thinking about all the negative consequences, that I stumbled upon a simple notion. *There are no negative consequences associated with not getting high.* Nothing bad is going to happen to me if I don't get high, if I don't drink or use. As elementary as this sounds, I had never really thought about it seriously. All of my decisions had been based on the premise that whatever I was going to do, wherever I was going to go, I was going to be high. It was as simple as that. I would learn later that my drug addiction impulses were situated in the same part of the brain that deals with base feelings such as hunger, thirst, and procreation—the basic drives necessary for a species to survive.

The addict's brain is such a strong and powerful tool. It has the ability to distort reality and manipulate free will. My brain was in a civil war during the early-morning hours prior to my departure for the States. I left Amsterdam with around twenty grams of hash. I had originally intended to bring some home for a few friends and keep a little for myself. I had been a pot smoker since high school, and although I had drastically reduced my intake over the past several years, I still liked to partake on occasion. I had smoked very little over the course of this trip, just one or two hits a day, if any. In fact, I had come to the conclusion earlier that week that, half the time, I really didn't even enjoy being stoned. It was okay if I was watching a movie in the hotel room, but the hash really interfered with me getting out and exploring the sites. I would get paranoid when I was in social situations or around other people. Even with all this, I was still trying to figure out how I was going to smuggle the stuff back into the States.

That's when I started to think of my new *no negative consequences* theory. There I was, telling myself, my wife, and my family that I was going to get clean, yet I couldn't decide whether to dispose of the contraband I still had with me. I had to do the right thing, so I went in the hotel bathroom and flushed … half of it. Take that, you addict brain! You can't control me.

I resumed watching whatever movie was on television and began idly thinking about the rest of the hash. What was I going to do with it? Maybe I could just smuggle a little bit back into the States. I remember thinking that it just didn't make sense. How would it look if I got busted at customs? I went back into the bathroom and flushed the rest, except for a few grams I had in my drum tobacco pouch. Surely it would be okay to bring this back with me. I remember my brain telling me that even if I got busted with it I probably wouldn't get into too much trouble.

Looking back now, the situation clearly was insane. I remember it being very humorous at the time. I can vividly see myself lying in bed laughing, laughing at how hard my brain was making it for me to get rid of those drugs. I reminded myself of my *no negative consequences* mantra and returned to the bathroom to dispose of the remainder of my stash. With a tear, a chuckle, and a flush it was all gone. I definitely felt some remorse as I watched the last of my hash swirl down the commode.

This tinge of sadness was overpowered by other feelings. First and foremost was the feeling of accomplishment and satisfaction. I had done the right thing. I had actually disposed of some drugs, some good drugs.

To a true addict, a drug is a drug is a drug, not something to be easily discarded. It was irrelevant that I very rarely got stoned anymore, or that my major problem was with cocaine. My brain was telling me to hold onto the hash; you never know when you'll need it. Furthermore, I was going to give most of it away to a few friends. I wasn't going to make any money. I simply viewed it as bringing back some souvenirs. My brain nearly had me seriously convinced that it was worth the risk to bring almost three-quarters of an ounce of hash through customs, so I could give some away to friends and have a little stash myself.

Shortly after the water tank on the toilet had refilled, I began to feel a sense of relief. I wasn't going to have to worry about customs. There was no chance that I was going to get arrested upon entering the country. I wasn't going to have to concoct any lies to explain why I had gotten unlucky again and caught another bad break.

As obvious as this risk/consequence issue may appear on its face, for me it was usually not a question of whether or not I should take the risk. The only question was usually how I could take the risk with the least chance of getting caught. My mind would tell me that I had to take the risk. The only questions were how to do it and what precautions to take.

I left Europe one week after my last cocaine use with the realization that I had anger and resentment issues. I also had a large amount of guilt stored within me.

On the brighter side, I had my new *no negative consequences* theory and a rekindled notion that it *was* possible to have fun and enjoy life without drugs. I was also somewhat excited to get enrolled in an outpatient rehabilitation program.

These are all baby steps in and of themselves. Even together, they may only have comprised a stride or two from where I was a couple of weeks prior. They were, however, a start, and some progress, two things which are necessary in order to get anywhere.

Back Home—Now What?

Stopping is just a start. Abstinence is merely not using, not drinking. All I had been doing was abstaining from one substance, cocaine. I had scratched the surface of a few of my character defects, but I was still unsure how to remedy these flaws. Although I had no idea at the time, things were going to start getting better for me at an astonishing pace. Like a lot of things in life, however, they were going to get worse before they got better.

Honesty, here I go. There's a glaring omission from my journal regarding my first night home. I've tried to forget about it, to block it out. I had tried to clear out most of the materials associated with my drug use prior to my departure for Europe. The drugs were gone, and I had disposed of my pipes and ancillary paraphernalia. But I did leave a handful of used chores—resinous filters from one of my pipes—behind, undisposed of. Why? No good reason, just my addict's mind, probably trying to plan my relapse for me.

I knew they were there. I'd be lying if I said that I hadn't thought about them. I had thought about the dilemma I would be facing when I got home. I figured I'd cross that bridge when I got to it. Bad plan! No plan! An addict is lost without a plan. There will always be something gnawing at us to go ahead and take that drink, snort that line, hit that pipe, or pop that pill. It's okay just this once, it's only a little. It can't hurt you.

I would be faced with similar situations in the near future and be able to make the right decision. On this particular occasion, though, I was practically defenseless. The part of me that wanted to have one last hit, to experience it one more time, was far more powerful than the sliver of me that was saying, no, throw it away.

I succumbed. The first part of the experience was nice, that initial few minutes. The brief euphoria was quickly replaced by the same old feelings of depression and despair, the ones always attached to smoking chores, the knowledge that this was the bottom of the barrel. When the chores were gone, there was no more. The feelings were significantly worse this time. Unlike times past, this was really it. I wasn't going to get any more. There would be no resupplying.

In a way, the depression was good. It reminded me of the self-imposed prison this drug had put me in. It reinforced my desire to quit. This lesson had taken less than an hour and I couldn't wait till the drug's effects were behind me. I took a Valium and smoked some pot, anxiously waiting for the waves of guilt to subside and the cravings for more to desist. Tomorrow was another day. I could get back on track. I could learn from my mistake.

My first few days back home were pretty good. I immersed myself in my kids. My son, two weeks shy of his second birthday, returned home my first full day back. It had been over a month since I'd last seen him, well over a year since I'd been a true father to him. He was young. He seemed to pay no mind to the past. He was just happy to see me. He'll never know how happy that made me.

My younger daughter would be celebrating her sixth birthday in twenty-four hours. The elder would be completing her first year of high school in two months. What, if anything, I wondered, do I say to them? Nothing, I will say nothing for the time being. I will be with them. I'll spend as much time with them as possible. They lived ten minutes away from me with my ex, but over the past year plus, I'd gone two weeks at a time without even speaking with them.

Children are so amazing. They are so innocent and pure. Now I was able to watch them, to listen to them and to talk with them, simple things that my addiction had prevented me from doing to any acceptable standard. I was able to begin to make good on the promises I made myself in Europe. I would be the best father I possibly could.

My mother was also in town for a few more days. How hard is it to alienate a mother's love for a child? I had managed to accomplish that feat. She had done everything in her power to stand behind me and support me, yet I had managed to thwart her every effort. When my wife and I decided to get clean again, though, my mother was the first one back in our corner. We spent some wonderful time together. I was able to talk honestly with her for the first time in quite a while.

To have the opportunity to renew these relationships boosted my confidence and resolve tremendously. It was the start of bringing loved ones back into my life. I was able to begin the process of making amends to those most important to me. I was also keenly aware of the fact that if I screwed up again I might not get another opportunity to make things right.

As much as I wanted to succeed this time—and with all that was at stake—I still didn't fully realize that the changes I was attempting to make had to be for me, and for no one else. I believe there was still a part of me that thought I was doing this, to some degree, for my wife. She was still in rehab. I think I still believed that she was worse off than I was. After all, she had a drinking problem as well as a drug problem. I could still have a few drinks, if I so desired. I could handle it. The same went for pot. A part of me still thought I might be able to do a line here and there. Of course, I would have to keep it quiet. I wouldn't want to do anything that would upset my wife's recovery.

Most people would think that after all I'd been through, doing a line would be the furthest thing from my mind. Surprise! I was going to test myself my third day back. A friend had been watching my car while I was out of town. He was someone who I did a lot of partying with, and there was a very good chance that he might not only have some drugs to do, but also some drugs for sale. I had to go get my car from him. Just like on my first night back, I had no plan of attack.

I began thinking over my options on the way to his house. I was pretty sure I wasn't going to buy any drugs, but I still wasn't sure whether I might do a line or two, just to see how it felt. That addict mind is always working, always coming up with new angles, always ready to trip me up. Maybe I was learning. Along with my options, I began to think about my *no negative consequences* theory. Where that theory was my first night back, I don't know, but I'm just glad I found it on this particular day. I made the right decision. I really got a charge out of it. I even tried to explain my theory to my buddy, to tell him how good it felt to make the right decision.

What I now know is that I dodged another bullet. Addicts have no business putting themselves in situations like that, especially early on in recovery. I was lucky. Maybe it's because I was still buoyed by the recent time spent with my kids and my mom. I don't know. Maybe it was just naïveté. At that time, I think I still believed all I needed was will power.

That was Monday afternoon. Tuesday would be a big transition day for me. Little did I know that in just over twenty-four hours I was going to be having what might be my last drink.

The End of an Era

I can't remember when or where I had my first drink. I can remember having the occasional taste or even a small glass of wine as I was growing up. These occasions were infrequent, and I can honestly say that I don't believe they had any bearing on my eventual dependency on alcohol and drugs.

I will never forget the first time I got drunk. It was with a cousin, when we were thirteen or fourteen years old. We snuck a six-pack of beer from our grandfather's refrigerator and proceeded to drink it on the back porch. It was an amazing experience, that giddy feeling, the surreal nature of the whole event. I wasn't hooked immediately, but it wouldn't be long until alcohol began playing an ever more important part in my life.

Friday nights, freshman year of high school, splitting a six-pack with a friend became the norm. It wasn't long after this that Friday and Saturday night parties became drinking rituals. I don't know if everyone was doing it, but most everyone that I hung around with was. It was the early '70s, so I can't say with any certainty that what we were doing was any different from what a lot of other kids our age were doing at the time.

I also started smoking pot pretty regularly around this time. I don't know if alcohol leads to other drugs, or whether other drugs lead to alcohol. All I knew then, and all I know now, is that a buzz is a buzz. Sure, there were differences in the variety of medications that I ingested, but they got me high. That's all that counted. It amazed me then, and it still amazes me today, how some people will try to differentiate between various types of drugs. It's only my opinion, but I think those people are missing the point, at least with respect to individuals who have a problem with alcoholism or addiction. It's true that there are more negative consequences associated with illicit drug use, but if someone is abusing a substance, whether legal or illegal, they're doing it for the effect the substance produces.

Anyway, that's how it started for me. It is not my intention to present a dissertation on the part alcohol played in my downward spiral over the next thirty years. There are most definitely times when I drank too much, way too much. There were also spans of time when I was able to drink in moderation, without any negative consequences. In fact, my drinking had been quite controlled and precipitated few, if any, real problems over the previous few years. It is for this reason that the events of that Tuesday evening and the following day are pretty amazing, at least to me.

I can't really remember anything out of the ordinary happening on this particular Tuesday. I made only one journal entry for the day, a little after nine o'clock in the evening. As I recall, it was a pretty good day. I spent time with my mom and kids. I was able to break away for a peaceful lunch by myself. I can remember taking lunch on the patio of a local establishment and having two beers (Guinness Stout) with my meal. I'm pretty sure I even failed to finish my second beer. No problems so far.

Since my mom was leaving the next morning to go home, out West, it had been decided that we would have a farewell dinner that evening. In addition to my mom and me, attendees would include my three children, our nanny, and my ex-wife. I know that I was feeling some anxiety as the dinner hour approached, but I can't isolate any specific reason for my feelings.

I assume that the uneasiness was a normal byproduct of my current situation. I was in the process of removing from my life a chemical on which I had been highly dependent for quite some time. I was beginning to confront many problems that needed immediate attention. I was preparing to leave for the West Coast in three days to see my wife, whom I hadn't seen in a month. Our telephone conversations since her departure had been a mixed bag comprising just about every human emotion possible. The uncertainty I had in myself bred uncertainty not only in my feelings for my wife, but in her intentions toward our marriage as well. I was insecure when it came to rehab facilities in general, especially the expensive kind she was attending. I didn't trust them. Lastly, I was about to have dinner with six people who were not only close to me but who also counted on me tremendously. Innocent bystanders who had become collateral damage as a result of my addiction. Other than that, everything was going quite smoothly.

The first thing I did after we arrived at the restaurant and my party was ushered off to our table was to find the bar. I ordered a jumbo margarita and pounded it right there on the spot. I'm not sure exactly why, but I felt as though I had to hide it. Maybe it was just old behavior, trying to get a head start before everyone else started drinking. I'm sure that somewhere inside me I knew I was going to have to stop drinking, or at lease be discreet, around my wife.

The dinner turned out quite well, and everyone had a good time. I had another margarita, regular size this time, with my meal, and my mom and I split another one before we left to go home. That was it, no more alcohol. I wasn't drunk; in fact, I felt quite normal. Maybe a little relaxed, but no more.

I was in bed by nine o'clock. I spoke with my wife shortly before that, and although she wasn't in the best mood, it had nothing to do with me. Nonetheless, I still felt very uncomfortable. My written recollections of the evening, of the entire day, don't reveal much. I questioned whether my wife and I would be able to handle the real world when she returned home in a few weeks.

I had encountered some tense, uptight moments during the day due to common, normal, everyday situations: cigarettes, printer, and copy machine problems.

I ended my entry that evening with the following excerpts:

Life is tough enough. I'm not even happy when I'm drinking!!

FUCKING PAWS![1]

It's turning into a pretty bad night. Why? I was so up earlier. I think I'm feeling [my wife's] poor mood, but it's more than that, booze, frustration, I don't know.

That's when I snapped. My new laptop of five or six months wasn't responding as quickly as I would've liked. I decided to see if it could fly, across the room. It couldn't.

That was the last time I had a drink. There was no big blowout party, no blackouts, altercations, car crashes, or legal issues. There wasn't even a good story to tell, except for my computer's aborted flight plan. I didn't go out with a bang. I went out with a whimper. Of course I didn't know it at the time, but I would start taking steps the following day that would eventually change my life in ways I never thought possible.

I have no journal entries from the following day, April 4. Why, I'm not exactly sure. Up until this moment, I thought I could recall the events of that day with a certain amount of clarity. It's only now, as I'm trying to prepare a written record, that I realize my memories of that day are more feelings and emotions than memories of actual events. I can't even remember how my mom got to the airport. What I can recall is anger, a tremendous amount of anger.

There is one thing I figured out, however, and that is the role that alcohol played in my morose feelings of the previous evening.

---

1   PAWS is an abbreviation for post acute withdrawal syndrome.

Not only was the answer in my gut, it was right there in front of me, in writing, my own handwriting. Alcohol affected me adversely. For how long, I don't know. From the beginning, maybe. It's possible. I don't know. Did it have a negative effect on me all the time? Probably not; at least I don't think so.

What I do know is that prior to drinking the previous day, I hadn't had a drink in four days, not since my return flight from Europe. I was feeling good, Tuesday. I drank, not a lot, at least not for me, and then I stopped feeling good.

Life is tough enough. I'm not even happy when I'm drinking!! I wrote that, Tuesday night.

I also wrote, *I think I'm feeling [my wife's] poor mood....* I was. There's no doubt about that. This was before I knew anything about detaching, as it pertains to codependency.

Sure, I was frustrated. Life is tough, it's not fair—so what? Whatever my problems were then, or are now, alcohol is not going to help them. If the night of the flying computer is any example, alcohol will surely exacerbate whatever problems I may be encountering. Besides, my way hadn't been working for quite some time. I needed to try something else, something different.

I had been exposed to twelve-step recovery programs for alcohol and substance abuse about a year ago as a mandatory part of my first rehab experience. I didn't really understand them. I thought I knew what the general idea was, but as far as paying genuine attention or putting any substantive effort into them, that was another story. Up to that point, it definitely was not my story. That stuff was for people who had real problems, not me, or so I thought.

I went to two twelve-step meetings that first day after the dinner: one at noon, and another one that evening. A couple of things happened. First of all, I must have been listening. Although I made no journal entries that day, Wednesday the fourth, I did write some thoughts down the following day. Most of them were quite benign, at least as far as sobriety and recovery go. I wrote about getting caught up with current events, what I had for dinner, being excited and anxious to see my wife on Friday. I did however write three or four lines pertaining to the meetings I attended, entries that amaze me when I read them. What surprises me is that in very few words I was able to touch on several areas that have not only proven to be very important to my recovery, but also keys to my newfound happiness and my newborn ability to cope with life.

Issues such as *control* and *my will* or concepts like *letting go* are topics that I know that I must've heard about at some of the meetings I had attended the previous year. Yet up to now I had no idea what they had to do with a program of recovery and sobriety. There's no doubt in my mind that I was thinking differently this time around. I needed help. This time not only did I listen, I was listening with an open mind. I heard things at those Wednesday meetings that made sense to me.

I heard some things I liked. I heard some things that gave me hope. I still had no idea what I was going to do. I wasn't even sure where I wanted to go. Was I through with drugs and alcohol? I had no idea. I knew I didn't want them around me that day. I was pretty sure I didn't want them around me for the next several days. This feeling alone was a new experience for me. I would soon learn that if I took care of today, tomorrow would take care of itself. Just as long as I didn't drink or use today, I had a chance.

Abstinence. Not only was it something I had never seriously considered, it was a practice I viewed as unnatural. It had never been an option, not for me. Why would I be considering it now? Even today, I can't say for sure, but I think it had something to do with that glimmer of hope I received at those first meetings. In order for me to have hope, however, I also had to have faith. Faith was a big word for me. What was I supposed to have faith in? It couldn't be me. I had already lost faith in myself, or at least I thought I had.

Even today, I have a difficult time trying to figure out what was happening inside me during this period of my life. There were things going on that I was unable to recognize. Part of the reason was that I was consumed with thoughts of traveling to California and seeing my wife. I can't even begin to express how much I missed her. I had spent a lot of time thinking about her the past few weeks. I had written her letters and poems; some I mailed, some I read to her over the phone. Our reunion was going to be great. I had plans. I had already lived out certain moments in my mind. Seeing her for the first time; that first kiss; that long embrace. We would get caught up on all that had been going on as we drove to my hotel room. It would be a romantic drive. I had it all planned out. I had expectations.

I also, at least temporarily, had forgotten some of the topics discussed at the meetings I had attended the past few days. Maybe forgot is the wrong term. It was more that I had no way of knowing how I was supposed to implement these nifty topics into my daily life. I had picked up a couple of tools but hadn't been shown how to use them properly.

For me, as with most alcoholics and addicts, control issues had always played a big part in who I was and how I would act. I never thought of myself as a control freak; in fact, I've always been pretty laid back. This doesn't mean I didn't have control issues. I've always had a desire to please people and to make sure they were happy. When things weren't going right, or at least how I thought they should be, I would feel I had some sort of obligation to remedy the situation. I thought this was normal behavior, nothing out of the ordinary. When I used to think of control, my own or another's, I attached a negative connotation to it. I viewed it as a type of manipulation, or trying to coerce someone to carry out my will. When I thought my motives were pure, such as when I was trying to make someone happy, especially my wife, I failed to view this exercise of my will as control. But we all have a right to be upset or to feel down at times. If I can do something to improve their situation and cheer them up that's great. If I can't, I have to let it go. I have to detach.

I am powerless over people, places, and things. I may think that I can control them. I may formulate expectations of how things should be, based on my actions or inactions, but if things don't go according to plan, I have to accept this. I have no other choice. I can't control myself all the time, so why should I think I can control others?

How would I react when things didn't go my way, when I didn't get what I wanted, when my expectations weren't met? How would situations affect me? Would I start to feel down or unhappy? Would I form resentment against someone or something? These are important questions that I needed to start examining. Luckily for me, I was going to get a crash course over the upcoming weekend.

Easter in L.A.

Finally, I was on the plane, wheels up, headed for the coast. My wife had entered treatment six weeks earlier. It had been almost a month since we'd last been together, a visit I was trying to forget. I had flown out to see her right before I left for Europe. At the time, she had two weeks of sobriety, and I was still using, not a good combination. But things were going to be different this time. I was feeling very confident. Not only did I lack the desire to do drugs, but any compulsion to drink appeared to be gone as well. I had gone three days without any alcohol, and I was feeling good. This abstinence stuff wasn't so tough after all. I had gone to five meetings in three days. I was going to make my wife happy, whatever it took.

I had texted her just before takeoff, to let her know my flight was going to arrive twenty minutes early. As the wheels lowered and locked into place for landing, I could barely contain myself. It was an unbelievable feeling of excitement and anticipation. I had been contemplating our reunion for several weeks now and had produced a vivid mental video of the occasion. It was going to be so romantic and emotional. I would rush into the baggage claim area, and there she'd be, standing on her tiptoes to better scan the faces of the arriving travelers. Her eyes searched the crowd, and then she'd see me. Her face would light up, eyes getting misty as we approached each other. Then the embrace, the long-awaited kiss, and sparks would fly. People around us would get a smile on their faces and a little envy in their hearts, wishing they were in a relationship like ours.

She wasn't there. I searched for my phone; no messages. She hadn't called. She was probably having problems getting a parking space, or maybe she was lost. She had just gotten a rental car a few days earlier and L.A. was a difficult place to get around, especially if you'd never driven there before. She would be here any minute. I just knew it. My bags arrived, but my ride didn't.

The excitement and anticipation that had filled me only minutes ago quickly began to dissipate. My positive emotions were replaced with negative ones: disappointment at first, followed shortly thereafter by feelings of anger and resentment. My own insecurity intensified the situation. How could she do this to me? This was supposed to be a special moment. I had it all planned out. Didn't she care about us? Wasn't this important to her?

My phone rang! Great, it was her. Actually, it wasn't so great. They would be there in another twenty minutes or so. *They*—you may be wondering who *they* were? They were my wife and a guy friend who was driving her. She said she felt uncomfortable driving herself. So much for the romantic drive back to the hotel.

At that moment I was depressed, angry, resentful, hurt, and very judgmental. Why? Because my expectations hadn't been met. They hadn't even come close to being met. Things didn't happen the way I wanted them to, and I was having a difficult time accepting this. At the time, I could have come up with many reasons why things should be different, none of them my fault.

To me, this is a wonderful example of how little control I actually have over situations and people. My will and my expectations don't mean much in a lot of situations, and there's nothing I can do about that. I can't control or change the outcome. The only thing I have any control over is how I let situations affect me, how I react to them. In this particular instance, I reacted poorly. I was being selfish, not necessarily in a bad or negative way, just not in the right way. I also lost faith. Things happen for a reason, because they're supposed to.

There was a reason for everything that happened that night, for my wife being late and accompanied by another person. I did realize all this eventually. It's reflected in my writings from the following morning. I think that this was the first time I was able to apply lessons I learned from a twelve-step recovery meeting into my life.

That Saturday-morning journal entry contains some interesting notes. Not only did I realize that I had been selfish, I knew that I had lost faith. I had forgotten that things happen when and in the way they are supposed to. I realize that this statement—*things happen when and in the way they're supposed to*—may be hard for some to swallow. Those in disagreement with this statement, who feel that something in their lives should have happened differently than it did, may want to try this simple test: try and change it. It can't be done.

I can wish that something had turned out differently than it did. I can hope. I can take precautions so history won't repeat itself, but I can't change the past. The only thing I can do is try and accept things and deal with whatever situation I find myself in. That's life, and life will continue to challenge me as long as I am breathing, until my heart stops beating.

That morning's entry contains my first reference to the "Serenity Prayer": "Grant me the serenity to accept the things I cannot change, the courage to change the things I can, and the wisdom to know the difference." I don't know how many times I'd spoken this prayer since I first heard it, over a year and a half earlier. The majority of the times the words escaped my lips were during my first rehab, or the occasional twelve-step meeting I attended from time to time. I know I had thought about its meaning on numerous occasions, but for some reason it had never quite taken with me. It seemed to make sense. It sounded great, but I didn't think it applied to me, at least not all the time. I was different.

I was beginning to notice things about me and the way I approached life. The mere fact that I was beginning to examine how and why I felt a certain way was extremely important. In the past, it was very easy for me to succumb to whatever the feeling of the moment was. I was beginning to develop some guidelines that, when combined with self-honesty, would allow me to examine my part in the way I felt at any given moment. These practices would eventually help me find a more consistent way to live my life. The last twelve hours hadn't been much fun. Although there were good moments, they were eclipsed by the extreme lows that accompanied them. The roller coaster ride would get worse before it got better, but now I can see that the lows were really opportunities to improve my approach to life.

It's easy to hope and pray for various character traits: patience, tolerance, understanding, or courage, to name a few. It occurred to me that the only way I could obtain such virtues was by being given opportunities to practice them. If I'm never put into a situation where I have the chance to exhibit these qualities, how will I know if I possess them? Life is the ultimate proving ground. Over time, I will be tested in many areas, and it takes time to become proficient in any of them. Unlike the scholastic endeavors of my youth, life is not a subject that can be mastered. I can't *ace* life. My best hope is that I keep improving, continue growing as a person. At least that's how I look at it now. It never stops. There's always room for improvement.

During my first week of sobriety, I thought I had it all pretty much figured out. I wasn't sure what my sobriety date was, but I thought I was close to acquiring the answers to all of life's questions. After all, I hadn't had a drink in four days. The last time I did any cocaine was two weeks ago, unless you counted the chores on the night I got home. Pot, pills, I was pretty sure that my last encounter with those substances was prior to my last drink, but don't quote me on that. The important thing was that I had quit, I was through, and I had no desire to go back to my old ways. I still didn't really have a support group, unless you counted the folks from those first few meetings I went to the previous week. I probably couldn't tell you any of their names, and I most certainly didn't have any telephone numbers, numbers I could call in the event I needed someone to talk with about my addiction. I heard those folks talk about some pretty cool concepts. I'm pretty sure I even understood a small portion of what they had discussed. I hadn't registered for an outpatient program yet, but I would get around to it. I hadn't forgotten about it. I was doing great on my own. I was doing this thing my way. I was still very skeptical of some of the high-dollar treatment centers out there, like the one my wife was at.

I had a lot of concerns. I was consumed with fear, fear over the status of my wife's recovery, fear of losing her, fear that I was going to do the things I needed to do and still end up alone. When people begin a program of recovery, it's imperative that they take care of themselves. Sobriety must come first. It must be placed ahead of family, friends, employment, finances, or anything else that gets in the way. This can be a very selfish concept, one that can be very difficult for others to accept. I know I didn't accept it, especially at first. I didn't accept it with myself, and I didn't condone it with my wife. After some time in my own program, I was able to understand the importance of this concept. It's really quite simple. If, for whatever reason, I lose my sobriety, I will lose all those other things that I'm trying to protect. Maybe not right away, but if I fail with my sobriety, I will eventually lose everything I placed ahead of it: family, friends, job, and, finally, my life.

I had to take care of me. My wife told me that, and her counselors told me that. Unfortunately, that wasn't the advice I wanted to hear. My wife and my family were part of me. I tried to explain it to everyone. Part of saving me was saving everyone around me. If I couldn't save my marriage, I couldn't save me. No one seemed to understand, least of all my wife. I would get so angry and frustrated with some of her comments: *abstinence isn't recovery, you don't have any tools,* and *I have to protect my sobriety.*

I wasn't stupid. I knew what was going on. Those bastards had brainwashed my wife. They were trying to convince her that she didn't need me; that she couldn't make it with me. It all made sense. I was a threat. I was doing this sobriety thing by myself, on my own terms. I didn't need a high-price rehab facility with its fancy doctors and counselors in order to get clean. They were preying on the weak. They didn't care if they destroyed a marriage and family. I felt unbelievably isolated at that moment. Unfortunately, my loneliest hours were yet to come, and they were just around the corner.

My suspicions and anxiety continued to grow as Saturday afternoon rolled into the evening. She had just completed the sixth week of her seven-week program, and I had flown two thousand miles to be with her on Easter, which required an overnight pass. This type of overnight release wasn't out of the ordinary, but it wasn't automatic, either. One of the counselors didn't think it was a good idea, so there were some back-and-forth negotiations in order to get the thumbs up. I'm pretty sure that the dissenting counselor's objections had to do with me and my rogue recovery program. That made it even sweeter when my wife finally got the go-ahead late that afternoon.

This victory seemed to lose some of its sweetness shortly before our departure from her compound. There was a potential, slight change in plans. Nothing big or disturbing, but her plans now called for her to return to the center by 11 p.m. I say her plans because this was her option. Apparently, my wife didn't know if she was going to be comfortable spending the night with me. Talk about confusion. We hadn't spent the night together in over six weeks, and now that we had the opportunity, she wasn't sure if she would be comfortable. I don't think it was because of intimacy;

we had taken care of that the night before. Evidently the problem was being away from her friends and her support group back at the facility. Although I could see how this was possible. I didn't understand it, and since I didn't understand it, it was hard for me to accept.

I grew more and more anxious as the night wore on. I kept waiting for my wife to gather her belongings and leave. I managed to contain myself in order not to spoil the evening. This was a step in the right direction: I wasn't reacting. I was waiting, trying to be patient. She stayed. We had a nice evening. We ordered room service and watched a movie. She dozed off early, and I got to watch her sleep.

She left around nine the following morning, with our plans for the day still up in the air. I was still having problems with a lot of things. She was anxious to get back to the rehab facility, which disturbed me. I don't know whether I felt unwanted, but I definitely felt unneeded. I wanted to be a part of her recovery. I wanted her to come to me for support. I think a big part of the way I felt was because I was looking for these same things from her. I was counting on her for support. I interpreted a lot of her comments the past few days as being unsupportive. In reality, that wasn't the case at all. I would begin to realize this fact as soon as I started to work my program for me, and no one else but me.

There is a tremendous bond formed between people who go through recovery together, especially in rehab treatment centers. There is an intense feeling of *we're in this thing together*. You share your secrets and fears as well as hopes and dreams. Past negative behavior, acts that have been hidden away, are brought out into the open. Human frailty is exposed, sometimes to a frightening level. But usually after a period of acclimation this is okay, because you feel as though you're with family. It becomes a very close-knit group. My wife's group was no different. It was also a group I knew I would never be a member of. I understood this and was trying to accept it. My real fear was that this group was going to replace me in my wife's life.

Even with all these negative thoughts occupying space in my head I was able to realize that there was nothing I could do about it. It was something I just had to accept, and I was working on that. I also realized that I couldn't control my wife or her thoughts, a fact that applied to her counselors as well. They could all think as they wished—over this I was powerless.

Acceptance became very difficult on Easter Sunday. As things turned out, my wife and I wouldn't see each other for the remainder of that holiday. We spoke several times on the phone. We were even supposed to attend a meeting together that evening. Nothing worked out. I had no idea what she wanted. I had no idea what to say. I had no idea what to do. I was completely and utterly lost. I ended up walking to a meeting a few miles away from my hotel that evening. I cried on the way there. I cried during the meeting. I cried on the walk home. I thought my marriage was over.

My wife had chosen to be with her support group instead of me; I knew that was why she canceled our plans for the evening. The problem, at least in my opinion, was that she didn't have the guts to tell me to my face. She made up some lame excuse about wanting to eat dinner at the facility because they were ordering pizza. I was crushed. The only bright spot out of that evening's ordeal was the fact that I went to a bar and had a cup of coffee. I had no compulsion to drink. This really surprised me. If ever there was a reason for me to drink, surely my current situation must qualify.

My wife and I had a counseling session scheduled the following afternoon, and, if not for that, I might have just left Sunday evening. I was feeling good about myself. I wanted some answers. I felt as though I was making good decisions, but I didn't sense that my wife was acknowledging this. In some ways it seemed as if we were in competition with each other. It was her way versus my way. We were battling each other instead of the real enemy.

This was probably just my perception of the situation, but it was an observation I couldn't ignore.

Monday morning arrived with no relief from the turmoil inside me. I had to talk to someone. I made a phone call to one of the counselors at my wife's treatment center, a gentleman I'd spoken with several times over the past month, someone who had given me sound counsel on those occasions. Once again he gave me great advice. My wife had a lot on her plate, he said. She was coming to terms with her problems and trying to find herself as a person, a mother, and a wife, any one of which would be taxing enough on its own, let alone in combination. The advice I received was really quite simple. Enjoy the time we were going to spend together later that day. Stay in the moment, don't argue about the past, and don't worry about the future. If things became difficult, take the higher road, don't react, and just let it go. Even though we were both struggling with the same addiction, all of our issues weren't the same. Being members of the opposite sex, we weren't going to share the same views on everything. Even though we were both trying to get to the same place, it might be necessary for us to take different routes.

Although we both probably felt some apprehension, we spent some quality time together leading up to our afternoon meeting. I was looking forward to our session. I had a lot of questions, and I was searching for validation of some of my positions. I sensed that this might be the most important meeting of my life, at least as it pertained to my marriage. Most of my anxiety stemmed from feeling as though I was going to be ganged up on, that it was going to be two against one. After all, I'd spoken with this counselor before, and I hadn't liked what I'd heard. I was forgetting the fact that the bulk of our previous contact, if not all of it, had taken place during my Munich monologue the previous month.

The meeting came, and the meeting went. It lasted a couple hours. I learned so much in those two hours. I found out things about myself. I learned things about my wife. I made new discoveries about our marriage, both where it was and how to help it progress to the place I wanted it to be.

It was at this meeting that I learned just how bad our communication skills had become. It was at this meeting that my wife told me how much she loved me and that she had no plans of leaving me. This is when I began to realize that I had to get well for myself, and that if I could be successful with my sobriety, a successful marriage would most likely follow. I was also warned that in the event my wife was unable to stay in recovery, I needed to let her go and focus on myself. We talked about so many things that afternoon. I took so much away from that meeting: thoughts and ideas that I would be able to cultivate and add to with information from future groups and recovery meetings.

All the assumptions I had made about this particular counselor had been wrong. I learned a lot about assumptions that day. I had formed a plan of battle and built an entire defense mechanism around certain assumptions that were at best severely flawed and at worst completely unfounded. This therapist had been someone I feared. I didn't think she liked me. I didn't think she cared about me. After that two-hour session, she became someone I not only admire but someone I thank in my prayers on a regular basis.

Everything happens for a reason. Things happen when they're supposed to. I'm not necessarily entitled to know why or when. I just have to have faith. I believe it's a necessity of life to be subjected to trying times. Adversity and pain can sometimes be our best teachers. They can help us with life's toughest lessons. To me, challenge and accomplishment seem to go hand in hand. If I'm not challenged, how will I know when I accomplish something?

I was taking the red-eye home that night, so I had a little over four hours to reflect on everything that had taken place over my time in L.A. On a scale of one to ten, I felt as though I was at eight or nine. That's not bad, considering over the past few days there had been times when I had felt as though I was in negative territory. I was excited and I was motivated. I knew I had a lot of work ahead of me, but I also sensed that I was on to something the likes of which I'd never known. Somewhere along the way I had become stagnant as a person. It wasn't just drugs and alcohol that had stunted my growth. They were merely symptoms of other underlying problems. I truly believed that I had unimaginable potential for personal growth. All I needed were the tools and some guidance. I had a real feeling that as long as I stayed sober, anything was possible. The key was staying sober.

My plane touched down a little after six in the morning. I was on the phone with my doctor later that day, making the necessary arrangements to enroll in an outpatient rehabilitation program.

I would be returning to California in three days, early Friday morning. This time, I wouldn't be alone. I was bringing our two youngest children, my mother-in-law, and our nanny. My wife would complete her program on Saturday, our son's second birthday. We were going to Disneyland! We would spend the weekend at Anaheim and fly home on Monday. This trip would be nothing like the previous week's excursion. There would be some moments of anxiety and some periods marked with fear, but they would be nothing I couldn't handle.

In the meantime, I had a lot of work to do. Fifteen or sixteen months of constant, almost daily, drug use scars not only the individual user but the location of the abuse as well. Our house was no exception. By the time we quit using, it was virtually impossible for me to open my eyes without seeing something, a trigger, that reminded me of my drug use. The list was endless: plate, cup, glass, straw, lighter, spoon, paper clips, hangers, screwdrivers, Q-tips, furniture, pictures, magazines, movies, water, and even air. Although you can't see it, breathing reminded me of taking a hit. I could probably come up with a drug reference for just about any item you can think of. For a lot of people, these triggers can cause big problems.

My wife would be leaving a sterile environment, one that she had lived in for the past seven weeks. She would be returning to a house that was the scene of many crimes. How she was going to handle this, I wasn't sure. It had crossed my mind that it might be necessary to move. That's no joke. Sometimes it's necessary. Before I called the movers, though, I was going to do my best to clean everything up—to remove or erase as many bad memories as possible. The bulk of my effort would be centered on our bedroom, since that was where the majority of our use took place. My efforts included a thorough cleaning, a few pieces of new furniture, and some rugs, lamps, and a couple of pictures. I even moved the furniture around so when she returned, her first impression would be completely different from what she remembered when she left.

It can be very difficult for an addict to transition back into the real world, especially after six or seven weeks in a treatment facility. These temporary abodes offer an environment of safety and support, coupled with a structured regimen of activities, elements that are necessary for successful treatment. As much as someone may be anxious to complete therapy and return home, leaving these safe havens is often fraught with anxiety.

There were a lot of things I couldn't change or make go away, but I was able to take certain steps in order to minimize the impact of my wife's return. The toughest task was the cleaning. It might seem silly, but it was necessary to inspect every nook and cranny, all the drawers and closets, the seams between the hardwood floors, shoes, purses, pill bottles, medicine cabinet, any place where a small rock or any illegal substance could have come to rest. Through the course of my efforts I did find three chores, those residue-laden screens, that I smoked my first night back from Europe. This time I was able to dispose of them properly with no inhalation problems. It was a good feeling, doing the right thing.

Heirs to My Throne

Our bedroom had been our castle, although as I look back now, it was more akin to a prison cell, one that I held the only key to. Throughout my heavy use period, I viewed it as my sanctuary. It was my happy place, where I was able to isolate and stay high for hours, days at a time. Comfort and privacy aside, one of the biggest reasons I tried to restrict my drug use to this area was my children. I had a huge phobia that they would come across some substance I was abusing and ingest it themselves. The fact that my fears were completely warranted was evidenced by the numerous occasions on which a casual *carpet safari* would produce ready-to-smoke remnants of my cocaine habit. In addition, no matter how organized or safe I tried to be, my supplies always ended up on my nightstand next to the bed. It inevitably became too taxing to have to go to the closet or into the bathroom to prepare a hit. It was so much easier to be able to comfortably recline with all the ingredients within easy reach.

For these reasons, it was imperative that I deny my children access to our bedroom. Not only was it unsafe, but kids had a tendency to interfere with my buzz. They required so much attention. There were most certainly times when I would've loved to have them in our room, or play with them in bed, but I was too afraid that something would happen to them. I really shortchanged myself in this area. I sacrificed a lot of tender moments in order to stay high. As bad as the situation was, I'm thankful that it wasn't worse, that I didn't waste any more time than I did.

My children not only deserve, they are entitled to, my time. The most precious gifts I can give them are my time and my love. I've always loved them, no matter how high I was, but I was unable to give them my time. It's not that I didn't want to; I was incapable of the task. I had to work. My addiction was a full-time job. I used to really beat myself up about not being there for them sometimes. Then one day it hit me. It's probably a good thing I wasn't there a lot of the time, not in the shape I was in. I think it's probably better that I sacrificed some quality time instead of letting them see me at my worst. Either way, it's in the past, and I can't do anything about it now.

My children are a big part of my recovery program, especially my two-year-old son. My two daughters live with my ex-wife, about ten minutes away, but my son is here all the time, 24/7, so I'm able to spend more time with him. It is truly a wonder to live with a child as opposed to merely taking care of him. Living with versus caring for—the terms may be mutually inclusive, but they most definitely are not interchangeable. Now that I'm sober, I can enjoy activities with my children with no time constraints, without worrying about when they're going down for a nap or when I'm going to get a break from them so I can get high. During the height of my addiction, I would *care for* my son. This entailed feeding and changing diapers—mostly just necessary maintenance. When we played, it usually wouldn't be for too long, because I was always dying to get back to my room and my pipe. I know this sounds terrible, but I couldn't help it. My actions were beyond my control. If I had drugs, I had to do them. If I didn't have drugs, I had to get them. It was as simple as that. That's addiction. At least, that was my addiction.

Things are completely different now. I don't just live with my son, I live life with my son, with all my children. I experience what they are experiencing through their eyes and actions. Now

I have the ability to grow with them and to stay young with them. It's a pretty amazing combination. I'm able to learn from them. They are excellent teachers on some subjects. By observing the way they live their lives, I am better able to understand and implement certain concepts that are a big part of my recovery program. Staying in the moment is one of them. I've already talked about how important it is to get out of the past. I have to let go of the incidents that have caused me resentment and anger. Additionally, it's not good for me to get too far ahead of myself, to project into the future. I need to focus on what's going on around me right now, at any given time. It's the concept of living in the moment, one that I need to be better at and kids seem to be so good at. The following chapter is an example of a lesson I was subject to about two weeks into my recovery.

Living in the Moment

I got to discover and enjoy something last night, a concept that I have occasionally practiced in the past and that is quite prevalent in much of the discussion and text that I have immersed myself in since I began my recovery. I got to experience firsthand a perfect example of living in the moment. Like so many of the ideas I am trying to incorporate into my life these days, this one is a combination of thoughts and practices. In order for me to truly be able to live in the moment in this particular situation, I had to also relinquish control or *my will* over the situation. I had to change my expectations of what should be for the particular span of time I was occupying at the moment. Bingo! Bonus points! I also realized that by taking these measures I was being truly unselfish. All this rolled in one—not a bad deal.

Our two-year-old son has been sleeping with us, and he hasn't been very cooperative when it comes to going to bed lately. Last night in particular, my wife and I had different plans than he did. Our intentions were to watch a movie or something on TV, maybe read a little or do some writing. At first, at least for me, his complete disregard for the hour and our desire for him to retire were quite perplexing, frustrating, somewhat annoying at times— and did I mention frustrating? Poor us! In order to coax him off to dreamland, it was necessary to turn out the lights, turn off the television, and feign sleep. All this in order to persuade him that he should make his best attempt to slumber off to wherever it is that two-year-olds go when they fall asleep.

As we pretended to sleep, he tossed, turned, wrestled with his blanket and pillow, sighed, mumbled, stretched, and relocated himself to all four corners of the bed. He bounced back and forth between my wife and me. He tried putting both feet in his mouth (his feet of course). Then and only then did he discover a position, one that he had already poised himself in several times earlier, and slowly began to drift off to sleep.

As I observed this, it struck me that, although highly unlikely, this could possibly be the last night he will exhibit such a propensity for ending his day and entering *night-night* time with us in our bed. I'm pretty sure it will be a while before he will prefer to retire to his own room in the evening and drift off in the solitude of his own space. For certain this day will arrive eventually, and when it does, tonight's ritual will be gone for good, never to return.

As an added bonus, I was able to lie in bed with my wife with no distractions, no noise but for the sound of evening's silence. I could actually feel the rhythm of her breathing, the complete peacefulness of the situation. I was able to lightly caress her shoulder, her arm, and hold her hand. She brushed hers against my arm, my back, and my hair, all bathed in silence, so serene. Resting, relaxing, states we so desperately search out once the sun begins its daily ascent each a.m.

I realized I was truly, unequivocally living in the moment, taking it for what it was and not attempting to control or manipulate it in the littlest way. I was enjoying it solely for what it was willing to offer me at that exact instant. I'm sure it will be impossible to extract such serenity and joy from all such moments in the future, but that doesn't matter. I know that after experiencing this particular event, it will happen again if I am just willing to let go, let things unwind as they are meant to be. Now I have a better idea of how and where to find such moments. They're everywhere, every day, and I don't have to prepare for them or take any action in order to experience them. All that is required of me is to be there, to immerse myself in them, to live them. I just need to be there as they unfold, relinquish my expectations, my desires, and my will over the situation. I need only take each moment for what it has to offer me, for each one surely has something it's trying to afford me if I can be cognizant enough to open my eyes, my mind, and my heart, and live them.

I've come to realize that living in the moment is much more than merely keeping my thoughts from dwelling on the past or projecting into the future. Yes, it's true that such mental training will undoubtedly stem most anger or resentment from past events, as it will quell potential anxiety and worry based on trials and tribulations that have yet to come. While this is a wonderful start, it only allows me to be alive in the moment as opposed to living the moment.

Life is a series of moments. When I use the new life skills I am acquiring to squeeze the most that each one of these moments has to offer, I'm finding that the present is usually very special and very rewarding. When I'm doing a good job at this, I'm able to string some pretty amazing spans of time together.

I've since applied the lessons I learned that night to various situations, ones that in the past would have caused me much frustration and concern. I've used these techniques in traffic, on airplanes, and in arguments. They can be applied practically anywhere. It's up to me. It's my choice.

There are still times when I find myself feeling completely overwhelmed. When this happens, it's important for me to try to identify the source of my ill feelings. What's bothering me? Is it something from the past? Am I worrying about something that may or may not happen in the future? Am I the cause of my discontent, or is it someone or something else? Is there anything I can do about the situation or problem, or are these matters beyond my control? These are important queries, especially the last one. If there's something I can do, some action I can take, that will better my situation, that's great, so long as my actions are appropriate and I'm doing the right thing. If the cause of my discontent is beyond my control, I have to get over it.

Sometimes I have a very difficult time detaching from situations that have hurt or injured me. This was especially true for me in early recovery. Everything was new to me. Life was different. For the first time in my life, I was trying to address adult responsibilities and problems without alcohol or drugs as a crutch. It's very important for me to keep tabs on where I am emotionally, mentally, and physically. When I encounter a problem or situation that bothers me, I need to find out what the root cause is and try to address it. More often than not, I'm letting things get to me that I have no jurisdiction over. When I'm confronted with a condition I can't remedy right away, I try to use another tool, one that I mentioned earlier: I pause.

That initial pause is crucial. Even if I'm boiling over inside, I've got to make an effort to insert some space between my thoughts and any reaction that might be ready to spill out of me. This is important for two reasons. First of all, pausing gives me time to think, and secondly, if I don't immediately react, I'm probably not going to escalate the situation.

This tool helped me immensely in my first few months of sobriety, and it's one that I continue to use. If I can put some space and time between my head and whatever it is that's playing with it, I have a much better chance of solving my problems. If I'm able to take a break from a trying situation, I can usually get squared away. If I examine the situation and am still having problems, I try to forget about it for a while and let time take care of it.

Time Heals

One nice thing about time is that it has the ability to fix things, to heal wounds. Maybe not all of them, maybe not all the damaged tissue or emotions, but most people would agree that time possesses undeniable therapeutic qualities. In most cases, any residual damage is probably due more to something within us—resentment, regret, the inability to let go, pride, ego, or sense of self. Whatever the reason, we tend to hold on to things, to feelings, especially when they're unpleasant or painful. One would think that these are the exact files that our minds would most want to delete.

For some reason, when these unpleasant memories are prodded and stirred into our present consciousness, we react with much more intensity than we normally would about other recollections. We surely enjoy good memories, but it doesn't seem as though we magnify them as much as we do the bad ones—particularly when it comes to memories of bad behavior. When our honor and integrity aren't under siege, we are more apt to just let things slide. But when we are hurt or offended, we seem to have a searing, almost uncontrollable—and at times most definitely uncontrollable—need to explain, defend, justify, or validate ourselves. I don't know if this phenomenon is somehow related to our *fight or flight* instincts, but something inside definitely causes this type of reaction.

In a perfect world, we might reverse the situation and embrace or emphasize the good times while disregarding the bad times. Not burying them, mind you, but trying not to disturb them. We know that they are there, so why not leave them where they belong and let time, that magical elixir, do its thing and heal those old wounds?

The fact that things get better with time wasn't a new phenomenon to me, but it hadn't been something I actively pursued. It more or less just happened. I would become a beneficiary of my own inactiveness. Even now, it's still a waiting game, so to speak. The difference between my past and present is that now I know that if I do my part, it's a certainty that time will do its part and make things better. I can actively employ time as a tool for better living. This realization, combined with an honest effort to avoid dwelling on troublesome situations, usually produces a much speedier solution.

I'm becoming more proactive with my problems as opposed to merely reacting to them. Self-examination and personal assessment are so important to me now. Whenever someone or something is interfering with my serenity, it's imperative that I take a close look at myself. I need to identify what is actually disturbing me and then determine what part I've played in the matter. In the past, my old behavior would have simply devised a plan of attack and set up a defense parameter around my emotions. I would put up a wall around my feelings and start firing shots at whomever or whatever was attacking me. I guess you could call that my *fight* response. When my brain would decide that engagement wasn't the best option, I would simply go into the *flight* mode and distance myself from the threat.

No matter what choice I made in the past, I was putting myself into a defensive position. Regardless of whether I fought or fled, there were certain similarities in the two options. They both generated anger and resentment, two emotions that are life threatening to anyone's sobriety. They were also both reasons for me to abuse whatever substance was at hand.

When I was a practicing addict, it reached the point where most of my fights and most of my flights took place within me. I didn't even have to leave my room. I could wage war against whomever I wanted, whenever I wanted, all from the comforts of my own bed. Just about everyone had wronged me, and there was no doubt in my mind that everyone was against me.

Needless to say, I don't do that anymore, or at least I try not to. A lot of things I now see in myself—tendencies and emotions, character traits that surface when I find myself in a difficult situation—are a result of the work I did in addressing my past. As I mentioned before, all the resentments I used to carry with me had one common denominator, me. I played a part in each and every one of them. Some parts were bigger than others, but when you're dealing with character defects and individual flaws, parts are parts. Maybe I was selfish, my expectations hadn't been met, or I couldn't control a certain situation. Sometimes the flaw was jealousy, insecurity, pride, or ego. It doesn't matter. I was usually involved with the problems from my past, and I will most likely play some role in the problems I'll encounter in the future. I didn't mention the present because it's here so fast and gone so quickly it's hard to latch onto. My problems usually deal with some type of anger or fear. My angers and resentments are a result of events from my past. My worries and anxieties are based on events that haven't yet taken place.

The moment is so important to me now. When I was able to come to terms with the past and accept it, I realized a genuine freedom. That was the first half. The second half of this past, present, future puzzle for me is faith. My ability to believe, to accept, that future events will play out as they are supposed to, and that I can control only my own part in the production, relieves me from the weight of the unknown. It's a lot easier for me to enjoy the moment when I'm not chained to the past and weighed down by the future. I understand that this can be a difficult concept, especially the future part of the equation, but in reality, what other options are there? I can't change the past, and the future will be here literally in the wink of an eye—and make no mistake about it, when it gets here, it's here to stay. Well, actually it's here to turn into the past, which is where it will stay forever. I'm not sure whether that last sentence made a lot of sense, but what I *am* sure of is that other than seeing to my small part in this larger-than-life production called the future, there's not a whole heck of a lot I can do about what's going to happen in the next minute, let alone the next day, month, year, etc., etc.

The path to addiction and complete dependence on one or more chemical substance, as well as the journey into and through recovery, is a very personal experience. There are probably no two descents or ascents that are exactly the same. We are all different, and we all have our own way of doing things. I believe this is especially true with recovery. The trip down was the easy part for me. If I was going to get out of and stay out of the abyss, I was going to have to do some work—a lot of work.

Recovery was a completely new landscape and a totally foreign language for me at first. I enrolled in an outpatient rehabilitation program and continued to go to twelve-step meetings. My outpatient program helped me accomplish a few important things. It made it easier for me to accept the fact that I had a substance abuse problem and that without serious personal change, I would at some point more than likely revert to my old behavior, regardless of how I felt at the time. It goes back to that *abstinence is not recovery* theory I mentioned earlier. Addiction was only a symptom of my underlying problems.

My IOP also gave me an instant support group. Even though I had been through rehab before, and I was regularly attending twelve-step meetings, I was a little nervous at first. I was the new guy in the group, and the bond between the other members was immediately apparent. Recovery groups are truly amazing: these mismatched groups of alcoholics and addicts band together for one common purpose—to get and hopefully stay sober. I truly felt I belonged in this new group halfway through my first session.

The other point that the counselors and lecturers tried to drive home every session was the importance of attending twelve-step meetings on a regular basis, and by regular, I mean daily. I was definitely ahead of the curve in this respect. A lot of addicts and alcoholics who enroll in a treatment program think that they're going to find a cure there. That's not how it works. The reality of the situation for the true alcoholic or addict is that there is no cure. Our disease will be with us until the day we die.

Treatment and rehabilitation programs are just the tip of the iceberg, the first step in the recovery process. They can provide a support group and some tools and point you in the right direction, but they can't fix you. There's a huge misconception out there, especially among nonaddicts and nonalcoholics, that rehab facilities can administer a cure for addiction. People are stunned when someone they know completes a program and then relapses somewhere down the road. Many times they're quick to attribute the relapse to the addict's lack of willpower or moral fiber.

Alcoholism (addiction) is a disease, like cancer, diabetes, or leukemia. It was identified and has been recognized as a disease since 1954. It has the same four components of other primary diseases: an etiology or cause; signs and symptoms; pathogenesis, or course that it runs; and available treatment.

The most successful treatment program for alcoholism and addiction is a twelve-step recovery program. It's not the only way, just the most proven and successful way. That's one of the reasons most rehabilitation centers recommend that their patients attend ninety meetings in ninety days upon completion of their initial treatment. I know I was no different from most addicts in treatment when I balked at the notion of attending a meeting a day for three months. I thought it was just some arbitrary number until a counselor explained it to me my last time around.

Habitual behavior, such as substance abuse, eating disorders, sexual conduct, or smoking, takes time to change. Ninety days of continuously modifying conduct is usually the amount of time required to get an individual on the right track. In addition to breaking an old habit, this type of commitment is important in forming a new habit—in my case, the new habit was going to meetings.

I heard an astonishing fact from a lecturer just the other day. He claimed that there are approximately four hundred different twelve-step recovery programs out there. I had no idea there were so many things a person could recover from. Furthermore, the only difference between these four hundred programs was the wording in the first half of the first step. Other than the substance or conduct being addressed, the programs are all pretty much the same.

Something else that sticks with me and reinforces my belief in these twelve-step programs is the fact that practically every specialist and professional I've turned to for help has given me the same advice: go to meetings. Doctors and counselors with years and years of education and experience would keep telling me the same thing: go to meetings. I'm confident that if they knew of something else, a new medical or scientific breakthrough or some other form of treatment for my disease, they would tell me.

It kind of reminds me of the guy who goes to see his doctor and says, "Hey, Doc, it hurts when I do this." His doctor says, "So don't do that anymore." My doctors and counselors were telling me that other than helping me with the initial patch job, the early period of abstinence, there wasn't anything else they could do. In their professional opinion, if I wanted to stay clean, my best chance was to go to meetings.

I was approaching recovery differently this time. There's no doubt in my mind. The difference was that this time, I really wanted to stop. I had finally come to the realization that I had had enough. I didn't want to control my use anymore. I didn't want to moderate it. I was, and still am today, pretty confident that I'm incapable of moderation. This being the case, I made the decision to throw myself into my recovery. If there was indeed a better way, I was going to do everything I could to find out what that was. It was worth a shot. I spent over thirty years abusing one thing or another. Besides, if the recovery program didn't work I could always go back to using.

I still think about that today, almost six months into my sobriety. Fortunately for me, things are working, but if they ever stop working, I can go right back out there. I could start drinking in a heartbeat if I wanted to. I'm sure it wouldn't take long to find some good drugs. I have the ability to make that choice every day. So far, I choose not to. There's only one reason for that: the stuff that I'm learning is working, plain and simple. If I didn't feel better, I wouldn't be here. I'd be out there, drinking and using.

I'm so grateful to be in the place I am today, living the life that I have. I think about gratitude all the time. Whenever I have doubts or cravings, or feel a bout of self-pity coming on, I go over some of the things I'm grateful for. That usually gets me back to center, or at least helps reduce the negative feelings I'm encountering.

Gratitude

Gratitude. I like the way this word just rolls off the tongue. This wonderfully important word, this simple noun, may be one of the most overused and under exercised words in our vocabulary. We pay it tremendous lip service, and although we may not use the word itself on a daily basis, it is something that should be practiced each and every day.

If we cut through the layers of protective coating that envelop our true, inner being, we realize this deep down inside. We know in our hearts that gratitude is not just a warm, fuzzy notion, but an actual feeling that we should practice repeatedly, every day of our lives.

One of the problems, at least in my experience, is that people have a tendency to be oblivious to the small actions, deeds, sacrifices, services that we should be grateful for. I wrote this piece on gratitude while enjoying a vanilla latte from a worldwide distributor of quality coffee products. It was prepared especially for me by an individual I'd never met or spoken with before. I like lattes. They taste good. They give me a nice caffeine boost. They have the ability to turn an everyday, ho-hum moment into one that's relaxing, sometimes peaceful and reflective. They make a span of time a little more special, and all for the cost of a cup of coffee, more or less.

I have to admit that when I was younger, I never thought that one day I would pay $3.80, plus tip, for a cup of coffee. I'll cover that in the chapters on *INFLATION* and *IDEAS I WISH I HAD COME UP WITH.*

My point is that I've tried to make lattes at home. I've got the fancy machine for it. I've got the coffee, the milk, the water, and all the tools necessary. But I just can't do it like this particular world-famous purveyor of caffeine products can do it. Besides that, it's a pain in the ass. When I come here instead, I can enjoy this moment without the prep work, the mess, the cleanup, and the headache. When you look at it that way, $3.80 plus tip isn't bad. I am grateful that someone came up with the idea (although I wish it had been me), invested the capital, and built a store on every street corner of the civilized world. Lastly but most importantly, I'm grateful there was someone friendly willing to work at this establishment, take my order, and prepare this fine, tasty beverage for me.

This event was so innately small in the macro scheme of things, like a bead of perspiration on a flea, if you view it from a global perspective. How many cups of coffee are prepared every day? Millions, probably billions. But this particular drink was unique. It was prepared especially for me. This tiny event made my day better, and for that I was grateful.

The American Heritage Dictionary defines gratitude as: "The state of being grateful; thankfulness." That's it. What a minimal use of words to describe a truly important noun. It doesn't read: small gratitude, medium gratitude, large gratitude, just gratitude. This is where we as a highly evolved species tend to lose our way. Somehow, many of us have gotten the notion that unless it's something *big*, no gratitude is necessary. At least it appears that way to me. We may say thank you to someone if they have performed a menial task for us, but this seems to be something of an involuntary response, a pleasantry. We say the words without giving the situation much thought.

We hold on to our gratitude like it's in limited supply, something we don't want to waste, when in reality there is an unlimited stockpile of it in all of us. The only decision we need make is when and to whom we wish to dole it out.

Personally, I've found that if I concentrate on the little things, I not only feel better about myself, but there is also much less of a chance that I'm going to miss the really big things. I will be more aware of the things in life that I should truly be grateful for, many things that are right under my nose.

The world is a fast-paced, complex dynamo. It's easy to get caught up in things, easy to overlook things. Everyone is racing around, striving to make the most of life and get as much as possible out of it. I've noticed in some instances that the more successful people become, the less likely they are to apply gratitude as deliberately and as liberally as is proper. This is okay. It's a situation we all have the power to remedy for ourselves. There are no directions for gratitude's dosage on the bottle. We must all develop our own recipe for its administration. If we can recognize this and follow through accordingly, we improve not only ourselves, but our little corner of the world as well.

By the way, if you are reading this, I am grateful to you. Thank you.

I was only about three weeks into sobriety when I wrote down those thoughts on gratitude. My addiction had transformed me into a selfish, self-centered individual. I had but one purpose, to get high and stay high. Nothing else mattered. The only gratitude I felt was when I had the necessary supplies to fuel my addiction, or when I was about to obtain those materials. I would get really grateful right at the moment I pulled into my garage upon completion of a successful drug run. It got to the point where I felt a sense of genuine accomplishment when I was able to complete a deal and avoid the authorities. As far as the really important things in life, the stuff I should have been truly grateful for, it was all secondary.

Gratitude is a daily experience for me in recovery. It didn't take me long to realize this. I'm grateful for all that I have, my family and friends, my home and my job, my dogs, for everything in my life. I'm grateful I don't have to take the insane risks that for quite some time were a daily ritual in my life. I'm grateful that if I don't use or drink today, I won't have to worry about going to jail. I'm grateful my kids won't have to see me stoned or drunk. I'm grateful for the people in my life who stuck with me and didn't abandon me, even when I abandoned them. I am extremely grateful for the new friends I've found and the new approach to life they're helping me learn.

I've also learned that although the dictionary defines gratitude as a noun, my life is better when I treat it as a verb. These days, I try and practice gratitude in my actions and in the way I live my life. I have so much to be thankful for. The best way I've found to express my gratitude for all that I have is by doing my best to give back to others, both in my actions and my words.

Put Me in the Game

The singularity of purpose that had completely controlled my life for well over a year had isolated me from just about everyone I used to associate with. If they couldn't get me drugs, or if they weren't going to do them with me, we probably weren't going to hang out together. I would occasionally bump into someone at a bar or the store, but those encounters were brief. I became particularly uncomfortable about going out in public after my first rehab. It was terrible. You can't believe the things people were saying behind my back. The rumors were running rampant all over town. Apparently, a lot of people out there thought my wife and I had a drug problem.

Still in a state of denial about the magnitude of my problems, I began to condemn those individuals who were circulating these untruths. I could really rationalize. I was able to convince myself that things weren't as bad as they really were. It was obvious that those near to me, my family and close friends, were mishandling the situation completely. In fact, their conduct under the circumstances was so reprehensible I felt justified in getting high. I had a perfect excuse. I was misunderstood, and I was being mistreated. How could they do this to me? [Pass the pipe please.] How can they say those things about me? [Give me another hit please.] What am I going to do about these rumors? [That was a good one, fill it up again.] There was only one obvious choice. I would just remove myself from everyone's lives. That way I didn't have to talk to anyone or try to explain anything to anyone, whatsoever.

In addition to the isolation that addiction breeds, the initial decision to take myself out of the game, out of life, was based mostly on anger, resentment, and paranoia. I'm sure there were some other reasons and feelings in there, but those were probably the big three. As time passed, even though I was still getting high, I began to think about people, especially family. Such periods of reflection were isolated and of short duration. It would be impossible for me to start interacting with others until I could honestly begin interacting with myself.

I started a dialogue with my mom shortly before my trip to Europe. I can't remember which one of us initiated it. I informed her that my wife was going back into treatment and that I was going to make some changes as well. Mom is typical of most mothers out there; all she wanted was to see me healthy and happy. She was overjoyed to hear that we were going to try and get right. Our lines of communications opened up immediately, even before I stopped using.

It took me close to a month before I felt comfortable enough to even think about interacting with old friends from my past, people I used to see several times a week, before my drug use became completely uncontrollable. My rehab program and the meetings I was attending were helping me understand who I was and what had happened to me. Whereas in the past I would try to either deny or downplay my problems, I was now becoming more willing to accept them. With acceptance I gained freedom. The first step was honesty. I had to be completely honest with myself. The second step was acceptance. When I could finally accept what I had done, and make peace with myself, I was finally ready to face the world again. I still had doubts about whether I would be accepted, but what people thought about me really didn't concern me anymore. I had performed so many mental exercises over the past year it was frightening. It was as if I had an emergency response team working 24/7 in my head, preparing conditioned responses and press releases. I had position statements and status reports on file in the event I encountered anyone from my past who had questions about where I'd been and what had happened to me. I had declarations of denial for just about any rumor anyone may have heard. I could not only denounce any negative situation, I could spin events to the point where it would appear as if I had been a victim of someone else's misdeeds. I was adamant about keeping everyone in the dark about both my addiction and the collateral damage it had spawned.

Denial is such a powerful device. I would deny and rationalize with my wife, and she was standing right next to me throughout the whole ordeal. I needed her to help me with my campaign of disinformation. She could say what she wanted about herself, but I didn't want her dragging me into her mess. I had a reputation and career to protect.

There comes a point in most campaigns of this nature when the messenger begins to believe his own message. I can't honestly say when and where this point was for me. Even now, I'm pretty sure that my addiction had me fooled very early on. In fact, I think it might have been the exact opposite of most situations in which repetitive dishonesty is involved. A lot of times, that initial mistruth—something we know is wrong or misleading from the beginning—is repeated so often we begin to believe it. It's sort of like embellishing a past act; after a time, the fabrications become such a part of the story that even the doer actually believes the fairy-tale. With addiction, the mind has a way of convincing you that everything is okay right from the get-go. I knew what I was doing. I knew how often I was doing it. I knew that with respect to getting high, everything else in my life was a distant second, at best. I still thought everything was all right. I just had to make sure I had the ammunition to convince anyone else who might come snooping around and asking questions. This is a lot easier to do when you have already convinced yourself. I really didn't feel as though I was lying.

I think there's another reason that I employed the PR department in my head for as long as I did. I had to keep it on payroll until I was really ready to close down the operation for good. I've talked about how my previous attempts at rehab were probably more closely related to attempts at controlling my addiction, as opposed to eradicating it. As long as there was a chance that I would be using, regardless of the level, I was going to need some good fiction writers up there to help me justify my actions.

This was a big turning point for me. I was serious this time. I was taking it a step further than just being honest with myself; I was going to be honest with everyone else as well. This also provided me a bit of a safety net. It would be a lot more difficult for me to go back out there after I had bared my soul, confessed my past misdeeds, and asked for forgiveness. Don't get me wrong, if I ever let myself get to the point where relapse is probably inevitable, that last sentence won't be worth the paper it's printed on. However, if I'm aware of where I'm at mentally and how I feel physically, I can think about my commitments at the onset of any cravings or temptations. Then my confessions and promises carry quite a bit of weight.

When I became willing to be true to myself and commit to a bona fide program of recovery, disclosure to others became an integral part of my revitalization. This doesn't mean I'm going around telling strangers and casual acquaintances that I am an addict and I'm in recovery. I share this information with family and friends, people who are close to me and are aware that I had a problem. This is an important part of the healing process for me.

I know people who are struggling in this area at this very moment. They are trying to find solutions to their problems without letting anyone know that they have problems. What an individual chooses to say and who he chooses to tell are personal decisions, ones that every addict must decide for himself. In time, these are decisions that will come naturally. For me, it was just a matter of accepting my situation and choosing a path that would make things better. In reality, everyone close to me knew what was happening. They may not have had all the details, and it's not necessary that they do. It's a big-picture thing for me, a macro view of my life. I had problems, this is what happened, and this is what I'm doing now. Anyone who really knows and cares about me seems to truly understand the amount of effort it takes to beat a drug or alcohol problem. The disease is so prevalent that just about everybody I know is either affected by it or knows someone who is affected by it.

I am blessed in that I have a wonderful family. They would do anything within their power to help me with my recovery. I guess I always knew that they would be there for me if and when I finally decided to straighten out my life. I can't begin to describe the emotions involved in my family interactions. It wasn't until I finally sat down and talked with my parents, my father in particular, that I realized what I'd put them through. When I was getting high every day, dying was the last thing I thought about. For my father, it was the only thing he thought about. My parents were just waiting for the phone call, the knock at the door: "My name is officer so-and-so. I'm sorry to have to inform you that your son is dead." Maybe it wouldn't be me. Maybe one of their grandkids would be hurt while I was under the influence. There were thousands of bad scenarios, a countless supply of horrible endings to my tale. While I was using I had no control over how my story was going to end. Even being sober, I have no idea what tomorrow has in store for me, but I've eliminated a lot of potentially horrendous endings. Without even realizing what I was doing, I've also been able to give my parents the greatest gifts I can imagine.

I approached all my family members by telephone first. It's probably not a good idea to just drop in on someone you haven't seen or talked to in over a year, especially when the last encounter ended on less than favorable terms. I needed to get myself somewhat straightened up before I could even attempt to talk to anyone, especially family members. My situation played out quite well. Between my outpatient program and twelve-step meeting regimen, I was really beginning to get a handle on a new way of approaching life. Not only was I seeing a difference in the way I lived and felt about life, but everyone I came in contact with noticed the change in me as well. Word traveled fast. It seemed as if everyone I talked to on the phone or saw in person had already heard from someone else how well I was doing.

I initially got and continue to receive a tremendous amount of support from everyone I encounter. It's an amazing feeling to have so many people pulling for you—even casual friends, individuals I don't really hang out with, people who are more friends of friends. There is such a genuine outpouring of emotion that sometimes I get tears in my eyes when I think about the sincerity and love that have accompanied some of the words of encouragement directed my way.

I'm not the only one getting misty eyed at some of these encounters. I made my younger brother cry. I'm two years his senior, and we were as close as could be growing up. As we got older, we went different ways—different jobs, living in different parts of the country. Like most brothers everywhere, we had our differences, but we were always there for each other. There was nothing that could break that fraternal bond, except my addiction. We didn't speak for over a year. He tried to call a few times early on, but I wouldn't answer the phone. The first month or two of sobriety, I still had no idea what I would say to him, so I didn't call. I knew he was waiting to hear from me. Mom had told me. I can't remember that much about our initial phone conversation, other than it went very well. I'll never forget seeing him again for the first time. He lives in San Francisco, I live in the Midwest, so it wasn't as though I could just run over to his house and say hi.

When I finally got the opportunity, about two and a half months into my sobriety, I arranged to have dinner with him in San Francisco. We made plans to meet at a bistro just up the hill from the Marina District. He got held up at work, so I arrived first. I chose a small sidewalk table in front of the restaurant, so I could enjoy the view and have a couple cigarettes while I waited. I was seated facing downhill. The Golden Gate Bridge was down and to my left, the Bay below and in front of me. I can't honestly say whether I had a straight line of sight to these two landmarks from my seat at our table. I was, however, able to observe my brother as he walked up the hill toward me. The space between us narrowed until it was replaced by a bear hug. He couldn't let go of me. He couldn't even speak. All he could do was cry, cry and squeeze me tight. I'm not sure how long this lasted. I know it was longer than most hugs last. I also now know what I had put him through. I hate to sound like a cliché, but it was as if I had risen from the dead.

That moment will be forever with me. It was a wonderful event that will serve as a marker of the pain and destruction my choices had inflicted on those around me. It also reminds me just how much my family loves and cares about me.

These days I surround myself with two groups of people: those who drink and those who choose not to drink. They all have one thing in common. They are all supportive of me and my choice to live a sober life. I don't have a problem spending time with my friends who still imbibe. The only thing that's different is the situations I put myself in. Some of my friends still drink on a daily basis. Nowadays, when I choose to do things with them, they are events or activities that aren't necessarily alcohol related. Golf is a good example. I've played countless rounds of golf with many of these individuals over the years. I'm at a point in my sobriety where it's no problem for me to spend an afternoon on the golf course without having a compulsion to drink. On the other hand, I choose not to hang out at a bar with these same friends, an activity that at one time was common for me.

It's very important for me to take the necessary steps to ensure that I don't find myself in a situation that jeopardizes my sobriety. I go out to eat a lot, for both lunch and dinner. I make sure that I always have my own transportation, or that I'm with a sober companion who can take me home in the event I feel uncomfortable with my surroundings. When my plans find me at an establishment that serves alcohol, I take care of my business and I leave. I don't linger. If I'm there to eat, I eat. If I'm there for a meeting, when the meeting's over, I leave.

In the beginning, I had concerns about what I was going to do for fun, or how I was going to spend my time. The truth of the matter is that my options are limited only by my imagination. I can do more things and go more places now than I could when I was drinking and using. I no longer have to worry what type of alcohol is going to be served or whether I'm going to have enough drugs to get through the activity at hand. I can go out just to go out. I don't have to go out so I can drink. It reached the point for me that drinking was the event, not the going-out part. I can see now that my old behavior was a very sad commentary on how my life was going. I had to change my perception of what was going on around me and how I was feeling in order to have fun, or to think I was having fun. It used to be necessary for me to alter my reality in order to go to dinner. I shied away from restaurants that served only beer and wine. I love to eat, but it didn't matter how good the food was; if they didn't serve vodka, I'd go somewhere else. It was insane. I was insane, but at the time I thought my behavior was completely normal.

My approach to life is so different these days. Activities and behavior that I used to deem normal are completely foreign to me now. Not only am I a different person, but the rapidity with which these changes occurred is almost frightening. I would literally wake up some mornings and feel as if there was a different person lying in the spot where I retired the night before. Whereas I used to dread the arrival of each new day, I now looked forward to it. It was no longer necessary for me to get out of bed every morning in order to close the blinds only to return to bed and bury my face under my pillow. I was usually up and about before dawn's first light. I was and still am eager to begin each new day.

I found a new faith in myself and a new faith in the world. I was beginning to come to terms with a newfound force that was greater than me. I wasn't in charge anymore. I didn't have to count on myself to make the world right. I was developing trust in a higher power, one that could manage most of the responsibilities I had burdened myself with for longer than I can remember. I was beginning to accept things as they were instead of trying to mold them as I thought they should be. I've heard it said that faith is a concept that is nebulous. That it's something difficult to explain, something that can't be questioned (in another person).

I would agree with the statement that it's something that can't be questioned in another. If someone's got it, they've got it, and I can't take it away from them. Only the individual possessor can relinquish it. That's probably faith's most powerful characteristic.

As far as explaining it, maybe I can't define it, but I can describe it. Faith gives me a feeling of *freedom*. Maybe I'm just substituting one nebulous term for another. You can't see freedom either, but most of us can wrap our minds around that a little easier.

I used to worry about *the haves* a lot: should have, would have, and could have. They don't bother me much anymore. *The haves* relate to my past. My faith allows me to accept the past. If I am going to truly believe that everything happens for a reason, then I can't worry about what happened in the past.

With faith, I can also believe that the future will unfold just as it is supposed to. As long as I try to take care of myself and do the next right thing as it comes along, I've done all I can. That's it! There's nothing else I can do. Keeping this in mind, it's important for me to do my best to accept what has happened in the past; to not be fearful of what may happen in the future.

Now that I've taken care of the past and the future, all I have to worry about is the moment. At least that's the theory. Control (relinquishing it) and acceptance are the keys for me. These aren't the easiest concepts to implement into one's life. Being open-minded and developing the willingness to try and exercise these theories in my daily life was a big step. After I crossed that threshold, however, the results were amazing. In fact, things were going so well, I decided to run a field test.

Acceptance

A little over thirty days into my recovery I found myself strapped into one of those aluminum tubes again, hurtling through the air. An old friend of mine had passed away suddenly. I was on my way to Phoenix for the funeral. What a perfect opportunity to test some of the theories I was learning about in rehab and my twelve-step recovery meetings.

Relinquishing control and *letting go, acceptance* and *living in the moment* had all been working pretty well on the ground at home, in Columbus. Now it was time for a real test. I figured that cattle-herd air travel would be the ultimate experiment. Down on the ground, I felt as if I still had too much control. Up here, where the air is rarefied, I would be able to add confinement, air marshals, flight attendants, and about two hundred strangers to the equation. Let's see, what else—tiny restrooms, uncomfortable seats, no leg room, and inadequate storage space.

My point is that with commercial air travel I would not only be constrained by the ever-present parameters that confront us on the ground, but by several additional ones that govern us when we travel by air. Some are universally imposed, such as gravity, others implemented and enforced by federal and international governments.

When I took a good look at the rules and regulations surrounding any commercial airline flight, I realized that I wasn't even in command of myself most of the time. When I fly I lose control of many elementary decisions, such as when and where I can sit, stand, walk, eat, and drink, simple things I tend to take for granted when I'm on good old terra firma. When I paused to think about this, I realized that even if I was incarcerated in a maximum security prison, locked down in solitary confinement, at least there I would still have the freedom to stand up when I wanted to, go to the bathroom when I had to. Not so, in the air.

To make matters even more interesting, my wife and I were flying on one of the airlines that don't have seat assignments, and, for the *coup de grâce*, we arrived at the gate so late that we were the last to board. Did I mention that my backpack was too big to fit under my seat? In my brilliance, I had stuffed it with two bottles of water, a couple of energy drinks, some sodas, candy, chips, beef jerky, magazines, toiletry items, and a rabbit's foot. I'm just kidding about the foot. I brought my wife. She's my good luck charm.

Anyway, arriving late was a touch of genius. That type of dedication assured us of having to sit in center seats for the short four-hour flight to Phoenix. Center seats, fifteen rows apart. We did, however, get to sit on the same side of the plane, starboard side if I recall correctly. This was important, though, because at least we both had the same view, which made comparing notes at the end of the flight much easier.

Finally, everything was in place. I was in seat 6E, by default. Of course, my backpack was situated above seat 17E, and my wife was in 22E. She had the sandwiches. She also fell asleep shortly after takeoff, so I guess I was destined to forgo eating. At least the drinks were keeping cool in my backpack, eleven rows behind me. It wasn't as if I was separated from all of my provisions, though. I did have my neck doughnut. I'm sure you've seen them. I think they resemble one of those yokes you see on oxen or water buffalo on the Travel Channel. They're great for keeping your head from flopping all over the place when you're trying to sleep in a sitting position. Unfortunately for me, however, I had no compulsion to sleep. I was too uncomfortable, wedged between my two new friends and neighbors, Bob and Bob's wife. Since space was limited, I was wearing my yoke around my neck. I just love making a great first impression. What a perfect environment to practice acceptance.

A couple of hours into the flight, I began taking inventory of my situation and how I had gotten where I was: no wife, no backpack, sitting between two perfect strangers for the better part of an afternoon. I realized that I couldn't control even some of the things I thought I was in charge of, things that normally wouldn't pose a problem. I had preboarded and printed our boarding passes the night before. That way, we would be able to beat the crowd and secure good seats. I had envisioned unpacking a couple of books, my journal, and a few snacks before takeoff. I'd have more than enough to keep me occupied until it was safe to get the rest of my stuff (iPod, computer, food, and other creature comforts) out of the overhead bin later. My plan was to basically camp out, get comfortable, and enjoy the flight. I had brought so much stuff to drink and munch on I would have been able to graze all the way to Phoenix.

We got to the airport early, so there'd be plenty of time to check bags and get through security. I had been so organized and efficient that we found ourselves standing at the gate with a little over an hour to kill before takeoff. I had it together. I had it all planned out. This was going to be a smooth flight. I figured that even though I had a backpack full of snacks and drinks it wouldn't hurt to have a nice hot lunch before departure. The restaurant was right next to the gate. How long could it take to grab a bite? Did I mention that I wasn't preparing the food myself? Apparently, the BBQ pork I selected was frozen or something.

Anyway, that's why we were so late boarding the flight. That's why we weren't sitting together, not even remotely close together. What a perfect environment to not only relinquish control of my surroundings, but to practice acceptance of my situation. What was really ironic was that I had taken certain steps to avoid the exact position I found myself in.

Suffice it to say, my expectations for the flight were not being met. In the past, I would have probably been miserable. I would have known no other way to handle the situation. I would have most certainly started pounding drinks as soon as they became available. Things are different now. Instead of choosing to get upset, I chose to make the best of my situation. I got to know my new neighbors. The old me would have made a few initial pleasantries and left it at that, not to be rude or for lack of interest, but because I would have been too uncomfortable with my situation. I would have been concentrating on all the things that were going wrong, instead of trying to make the best of them. I would have fought my situation instead of accepting it. The gentleman I was seated next to, Bob, and I had some common interests. We talked about World War II aviation, air shows, and travel in general.

In the past, I've found it difficult to sleep on airplanes unless I was drunk or drugged. Strangely enough, about forty-five minutes into the flight I was able take a nap. I woke up a bit later and found it possible to make my way aft to recover my backpack. I somehow managed to cram my bag down under my legs in front of my seat. After a bit of maneuvering, I got my computer out and set up in front of me on my tray table. I was ready to type. The only problem was that I didn't have enough elbow room. There would be no computing on this flight. I reversed my previous maneuvers and got my computer back in my pack and settled for what was available. I listened to music and wrote for the next couple of hours. I read a little. Before I knew it, we were getting ready to land.

This is no bull. My four plus hours on this flight seemed to fly by. Not only that, I felt great. I've gone through back surgery and knee surgery, and long flights are usually hell on my body. That wasn't the case this time. I wasn't sore. I wasn't stiff. I wasn't tired. It was actually one of the most enjoyable flights I've ever had. Why? The only explanation I can come up with is that I was willing to accept my situation and make the most of each moment.

I do my best to practice these principles as much as possible, for the simple reason that they work. My flight to Phoenix gave me the opportunity to take a situation that in the past would have been tremendously frustrating and aggravating and transform it into a pleasurable experience. By making the best out of each moment during that long flight, I was able to do more than just pass time. I was able to enjoy the time. Such an outcome would have been impossible for me if I had simply battled the events and my environment the moment they began to deviate from my script.

The more I'm able to practice acceptance in my daily affairs, the easier it is for me to truly observe just how spontaneous life really is. I used to spend way too much time worrying about why things were happening in a certain way, and what I could do to control them, instead of accepting things as they were and doing the best with what I had in front of me. When I was drinking and using, I was usually at odds with what was going on around me. In reality, that's a perfect scenario for an alcoholic or an addict. It provides us with another excuse to get drunk or high, because things aren't going right, or we are having a bad day.

I never used to equate control with expectations. I thought for me to be in control of something, I had to be pulling some levers or yanking some strings. I thought that I had to be trying to physically control someone or something. With expectations, although I might not have my hands on the dials, I've got some idea of how I want things to turn out or how I want someone to act. When I'm expecting something, I'm projecting my will into the future.

I have to be careful with my expectations, because things don't usually turn out as planned, and more often than not, people don't act the way I would like them to. This being said, it's all right for me to have expectations, I just have to be flexible and accepting when everything goes to hell. The important thing is how I act when my expectations aren't met. On occasion, I've been told not to get my hopes up; that way I won't be disappointed. In such situations, hope is really just another word for expectation. Expectations are part of life, especially with those close to us.

Higher Standards

When I look at that simple noun with its simple modifier—higher standard—I think I see my problem. Whenever I try to impose any type of standard on another individual, all I'm really saying is that I have expectations. Whenever I do that, I'm setting myself up for disappointment. People are not like commodities. Unlike gasoline or meat, there are no different grades to choose from. I don't have the option of choosing between regular, premium, or high test. There is no official regulatory agency that can stamp people *prime cut,* or *USDA choice.* There are no guidelines imposed by other entities to assure me that whoever I'm dealing with is genuine, the real deal, or trustworthy. I have to make these determinations on my own.

In theory, I like to say that I trust everyone equally, but that's not true. People who are near to me, close friends, family members—I trust them differently than I do the casual passersby on the street. Am I supposed to? I don't know. The Bible would have me love my neighbors as I love myself. Let's be real. That's one lofty expectation. What about strangers, people I just met? Surely I'm not supposed to, not expected to, afford them the same treatment and understanding that I would my mother, my father, my wife and children. That would be preposterous. Wouldn't it? The golden rule is a nice guideline. I would like to think that others are going to treat me the same as they would like to be treated;

however, I can't count on that. What about my family? Shouldn't I be able to expect that from them? Maybe, maybe not.

I don't set standards for people. If I don't have expectations, I can't be disappointed. If something good arises from my interaction with someone, that's a bonus. I know this sounds cynical. Believe me, I'm writing this stuff down and part of me is going, wow, you're really messed up. This approach gets a little more difficult for me when I'm dealing with family. With strangers, acquaintances, and casual friends, I can usually get by without expecting much from them. But my family, that's the heart and soul of my existence. I can't help but have some level of expectations, some minimal standards that I believe they should adhere to.

I should mention at this point that I'm hurting today. In fact, my mood and emotions are what led me to this topic. That's why I'm writing about it. I feel as though I've been let down, treated poorly, by someone close to me. Not by anything that person may or may not have done, but by the manner in which she conducted herself toward me. I could be wrong about the entire matter, but I don't feel as though she was completely honest with me. I feel she's omitted or manipulated communications in order to hide something from me.

I know I have no control over this individual, that this person loves me dearly, and that she has problems and issues of her own. I know all that, but I still feel let down, almost betrayed, to the point where I don't even think I can discuss the situation.

That's *my* problem. I let myself get to this point. Were my expectations too high? Were the standards and loyalty I imposed (self-imposed) upon this person too lofty? I don't know. The simple fact is that I put them in place—the expectations, that is. It's up to me to cope with the situation. I am the only one who can make me right. I think I expect too much sometimes.

I know that I've been at fault for such things in the past, things I've done that are comparable to the things that are bothering me this very moment. I do think it's important for me to accept and to forgive, because I know this person really didn't mean to act the way she did. She may not have even realized it, and if she did, she probably didn't have much control over the situation at the time. These things happen sometimes. We are all flawed. We are human. I know that I can't dwell on it. I have to move on and get right with it. I'm pretty sure that time will help erase the feelings I now have. I'm fairly certain that the issue will be discussed at some point in the not-too-distant future, maybe not the immediate future, but soon. I want to cope with it and get over it, because I don't like the way I feel right now. Things are already better than they were a couple of hours ago. There was a period of time earlier when I know I could have let the incident develop into real anger. I'm pretty sure that that period has passed, and that anger isn't an option. I'm glad I checked myself. I listened to my thoughts on the matter and really examined them internally, instead of just reacting to them. This was a good move on my part. The old me would have surely turned the situation into something ugly. Regardless of the validity of my position, I'm learning that there's not much use in going to that dark place, a location where I used to find myself quite often. I know that I have to try and understand, be compassionate, and most importantly to forgive. This person may need me now more than ever.

I wrote this last section about two months into my sobriety. It was about a month after my trip to Phoenix, the one where *letting go* and practicing *acceptance* turned what could have been a miserable situation into a wonderful experience. In this particular instance, my wife was not meeting my expectations of how I thought she should be behaving. As I wrote above, it wasn't as though she was doing anything to me. It was the way she was acting. Another one of our friends had recently died suddenly. It was difficult for everyone involved. I was trying to be both compassionate and empathetic toward her situation, but some of her behavior was still bothering me. This event proved to be another learning experience for me.

There was nothing wrong with my expectations so long as I was able to handle the situation in an appropriate manner. My concerns were centered on how she was handling her grieving process, who she was hanging around with, and where she was spending her time. We were eventually able to discuss the situation and sort everything out. In addition to teaching me another lesson in control and acceptance, the events served as a reminder that I can't work someone else's program for them. How they choose to handle their recovery is their business, not mine. I can only work on me.

Almost three months have gone by since I wrote about higher standards and the expectations I place on those close to me. As I become better equipped to handle life and practice acceptance, I find I'm not as cynical as I was such a short time ago. It's completely normal for me to have certain expectations about people, even strangers. If I decide to get in my car and leave the house, there's a pretty good chance I'm going to interact with other motorists out on the road. I can assume that they're going to operate their vehicles in a safe and courteous manner. In reality, though, I know that's not going to be the case. If it were, the term road rage would never have been invented. This is an elementary example of a much more important point. Expectations aren't the problem. It's how I deal with an unfulfilled expectation that counts.

Sometimes I find myself in situations where no matter how hard I try, acceptance still eludes me. In these cases, I have another weapon in my arsenal that I can use to help me battle frustration, anger, and resentment: tolerance. I used to think tolerance and acceptance were interchangeable. Now, however, I view tolerance as being a few degrees short of acceptance. To tolerate connotes to put up with. I don't have to approve of someone or something. I don't necessarily have to accept the situation either. As long as I'm able to tolerate the situation, things will generally work out okay.

As with so many positive character traits, patience is a cornerstone of tolerance. The more patience I can muster, the more able I am to practice tolerance. I've found that there's a bit of a step-by-step process involved here. If I can be tolerant, then I have a chance at moving on to acceptance. In many instances, the only difference between tolerance and acceptance is time. After some time passes after my initial decision to be tolerant, and I have an opportunity to think the situation over, I'm better able to understand someone else's position or thinking. I realize that I was letting my will and my expectations get in the way of the situation, instead of truly being open-minded about it.

I can make life as complicated as I choose to. Conversely, I can make things a lot easier on myself as well. When I was out there trying to call the shots and control life, not just my life, but everything that affected it, things usually didn't work out, at least not as I thought they should. A lot of times, when things didn't go the way I thought they should, my self-will seemed to turn into self-pity. Poor me! How can this be happening to me? Life isn't fair.

Don't get me wrong, I didn't think like this all the time. I'm a very fortunate person, and I've been blessed with a great family and many resources. I was always aware of this, but at the height of my addiction I lost my focus, and my priorities were really jumbled. I used to think I should be able to live my life as I pleased. If this included getting high every day, so be it. As I mentioned earlier, I used to think that if I were content to completely neglect my obligations to everyone and everything around me, then I had a right to do so. In fact, that's exactly what I did for a while. The problem was that I didn't have a right to neglect my family and children, not unless I was willing to pay the consequences for such action. I used to think I was entitled to certain treatment and certain things. I think I now have a better understanding of what my true rights are.

Inalienable Rights

The term is in the Declaration of Independence, but our founding fathers use the prefix un-, as opposed to in-. I know this because I had to check it on the Internet. I was pretty sure the term was in the Declaration of Independence, but I wasn't positive. I actually checked the Constitution and the Bill of Rights first. Inalienable rights, it's a term I hear from time to time, but I think our Declaration is the only place I've ever actually seen it written.

What are they? What do they mean? I never really thought about it much. I guess I just assumed the term meant I was free; that I have freedom, whatever that means. Until this morning. I was sitting outside as usual, thinking about smoking a cigarette and enjoying the morning. I realized that that was it. These were my inalienable or unalienable rights. These simple items that my Higher Power gave me, and my country's Constitution and its Bill of Rights promise to protect for me. Among these rights are life, liberty, and the pursuit of happiness. On their face, these don't guarantee me much, but at the same time, they guarantee me just about everything.

To me, they are simple rights that allow me to do as I please. That's the key, that's the magic in them. I can do as I choose to do because of them, no more, no less.

I was free to wake up at 5:30 a.m.; to sit outside and meditate, pray, and contemplate the day that lay before me. What was I, as a person, going to do with them?

I have some work to do—writing, going to meetings, and spending more time with my family, and whatever else I decided I wanted to do today. I can choose to do what's right. I can choose to do what's wrong. It's up to me. I can seek guidance about what I want to tackle today. I can decide on my own. It's basically all up to me.

That's what my inalienable rights are. No person, no entity promises me that I'm going to be happy today. That's my choice. No one is guaranteeing me a paycheck today. That is my choice as well. I have a roof over my head. I have food in the refrigerator. As basic as it sounds, there were times when I took these things for granted. Freedom, food, shelter—I thought I was entitled to them. I'm not.

The freedom to do as I wish is crucial. Without it, I may not be able to acquire food and shelter and the other things I want out of life. A couple of days in jail opened my eyes to that. I stepped out of line and lost my freedom of choice for a weekend. I still had food and shelter, but the shelter wasn't comfortable, and I had to eat the food when I was told to.

That was six months earlier, and at the time I really didn't get it, about inalienable rights. I didn't understand how simple it really was. I think I get it now. If I do the right things, the really big ones—more precisely, if I avoid the wrong decisions, the ones that end up getting me locked up somewhere—then I have the opportunity to do with my life as I please.

It's up to me to be happy, or unhappy, and it really shouldn't matter what material things I have. Regardless of what my possessions are, if I have my freedom, my inalienable rights, I have an opportunity to do or become just about anything I choose. This doesn't necessarily mean that I'm going to become a professional athlete or a famous movie star. If I lack speed and agility, or if

I'm extremely camera shy, these professions probably wouldn't be right for me. That doesn't mean I can't work in the sports or film industries in some other capacity. I just need to determine what my strengths are and take it from there. If something's meant to be, it will happen. How do I know this? I have faith.

Drinking and drugging really wreaked havoc on my faith. Not so much at first, but as my disease progressed, my faith was transformed more into something along the lines of *wish*. I wished things. Boy, I wish this would happen, or I wish that hadn't happened. Toward the end, I really didn't even wish very much. Life just kind of moved on; another day, another $300 or $400 in supplies. It was pretty much the same routine day in and day out. That's how it was when I was in charge of things. I couldn't look past today to see tomorrow.

Shortly into sobriety, it became apparent that I was going to have to vacate the driver's seat. It's a good thing I was able to realize this, because that's not always the case. Having the desire to quit is a great start, but it takes more than that to stay sober, at least in my case. If desire were the only requirement, I would have been able to quit a couple times.

There are a few similarities in my previous attempts at stopping, ones that are common among a lot of alcoholics and addicts. My continuous pattern of abuse would beat me up and beat me down to the point where I knew I had to do something about it. I believed I had the power to change things. I could and I did, but it was always for a very short time. As soon as I was feeling good again—which was usually only a couple of days—I'd be back at it. I believed that I was the master of my universe and that I had complete control over everything. When I did have faith, I had faith in myself, and only in myself.

It's amazing how fast this disease can break a person down. When I finally reached the point that I had no faith in myself or anything in my life, I began to look outside the box. By box, I mean the self-constructed, self-imposed, and self-administered space in which I was living my life. That's where my ability to run things had gotten me. I wasn't sure if there was a way out, but I figured I might as well try something different.

Higher Power

I think it was more of an instinct than a conscious thought, but when things were at their worst, I found myself praying for help. It was really no big surprise. I had done it before, especially when I would find myself in a tight spot. These periodic requests for divine intervention usually involved relationship and financial problems. I think I almost always tried to bring God with me when I went to Las Vegas. I also have several vivid recollections of trying to contact him when my team was having difficultly covering a point spread. Of course, I know he's a busy guy, so I didn't bother him unless it was a substantial wager. I'm pretty sure I usually promised him something in exchange for his assistance. I'm also pretty certain that on those occasions when he came through for me, I failed to keep my end of the bargain.

Before going further into the subject, let me stress the point that I'm not going to try to help you find Jesus or save your soul. I'm not going to try to show you the way or point you in a specific direction. Spiritual belief of any kind, or lack of belief therein, is an extremely personal issue. I've always had a problem with individuals and organizations that try to tell me that their particular denomination has all the answers. In fact, I find it offensive and arrogant when someone tries to sell me on the notion that not only is their way the right way, it's the only way.

The important thing isn't what you believe in, it's that you believe in something. As far as I'm concerned, it's completely up to the individual. I don't care whether you believe in God, Allah, Buddha, or the giant oak tree in the backyard. It's important for me to believe in a *Higher Power*, something greater than myself, for the simple reason that I've already proven that I can't do it by myself.

I've heard people say they consider their support group to be their higher power. There are others who believe in merely aspiring to move forward with their lives in a good, orderly direction. It may be as simple as making a conscious effort to do the next right thing. In the beginning, the important thing is to have something to latch onto, something to have faith in. The relationship may grow and eventually evolve into something bigger. Some individuals may already have a relationship with a Higher Power when they enter recovery. If so, over time, the relationship may stay the same, or it may change. It all depends on the individual.

In my case, I've always believed in God. That didn't necessarily mean I knew how to define my relationship with my Higher Power. I've always had difficulty with what to think and what to believe when it comes to religion. I know I've always believed in spirituality at some level, but I also believe in science. The two camps have always seemed to be at odds. There were many times when I felt that if I believed in one I couldn't believe in the other.

Now I've found that, at least for me, there's room for both. I can believe in evolution and the Big Bang theory. For me, that explains how we got to where we are today. However, there's a bigger question that science can't answer. Where did all the gas and debris, the building blocks of the universe, come from? How did these materials get here? That's a faith question.

Part of my problem in the past was that I was moving too fast. I wasn't paying attention to the details of the events going on all around me at any given moment. I was either upset about something that had happened in the past, or I was worried about what was going to happen in the future. There are miracles, things that occur on a daily basis, that I'm much more in tune with these days.

Sunrise is one of my favorites. Planetary rotation, orbital plane around the sun, mathematics, and physics, I know about all the scientific explanations. I took fifteen hours of astrophysics and geophysics in college. I watch the History Channel and the Discovery Channel. My knowledge does not diminish the fact that each sunrise is a miracle in and of itself. The fact that our planet can sustain life at the level it does is amazing. Whether you choose to believe in evolution or creationism, human beings are miracles.

Children, especially babies, are miracles. If you don't have children, you may not quite understand the magic involved with the birth of a child. I don't care how scholarly or scientific a person is. I've yet to meet a parent who has the ability to simply brush off the birth of a child as being merely a biological process.

Science answers a lot of questions. It can explain many things, but it can't explain everything. That's where a little bit of faith can go a long way. The more I think about it, the more I believe that science and religion are a perfect match. Some things just can't be explained by a scientific theory, or anything else for that matter. What's wrong with using faith to fill in the blanks?

Coincidence and luck are two other explanations that get tossed around a lot when there's no other readily available answer. What is coincidence? What is luck, good or bad? Science is based on mathematics. I don't ever recall seeing the terms coincidence or luck in a mathematical equation. Is it possible that there is no coincidence or luck? That the events we attribute these terms to are really part of a bigger, overall plan for things? It's just something to think about. It's a question for individuals to ponder on their own terms.

My faith also helps me cope with the world when things don't go my way. When I have faith and can believe that everything happens for a reason, it's easier for me to relinquish control. As long as I have faith in something besides myself, I always have a place to go for advice. My faith is my faith. My beliefs are my beliefs; they're personal to me.

You may not believe in my beliefs. You may have your own. That's what's so great about faith and beliefs in a Higher Power. They can't be proven, at least not realistically, not with concrete, indisputable evidence. People may think they have such proof, but what they really have is faith. They have faith to the point of being convinced that they have found something, seen something, or heard something that proves beyond any doubt that their Higher Power is tangible and real.

If I am to believe that there is a universal plan and that everything happens for a reason, it's imperative that I have faith. This belief is an important step for me, because it allows me to get out of the way. Faith allows me to place the collective blueprint ahead of my will. When I put my will, what I want, ahead of everything else, a couple of things can happen. The first is that I create a situation in which I may act selfishly. When this happens, and my expectations aren't met, there's a good chance that I'm going to get either disappointed or upset, neither one of which is a good emotion for alcoholics or addicts. These emotions give us another excuse to escape to alcohol or drugs.

When I have regular contact with my Higher Power, it's easier for me to set my will aside. I pray differently than I used to. I don't ask for things anymore. Now I ask for guidance. Since I made this change, I've had some amazing results.

When I ask what I should do in a situation, as opposed to telling God what I want, I usually get an answer. It's not a booming voice from above. The ground doesn't shake. I don't see signs or any outward signals. The answer usually comes from within. I almost always know what the right thing to do is. I think I'm able to find the answers now because I'm seeking direction instead of asking for a specific outcome.

When I used to pray for a particular result, I had already made my mind up about what I wanted. I was asking a divine entity to grant me my will. It didn't matter what was right or what was wrong; the only thing that was important to me was getting my way. Nowadays, I just want to get out of the way and try to do what's right. I'll be the first to admit that I'm not always successful at it. When I'm willing to seek guidance so that I may carry out my Higher Power's will, as opposed to my own, I'm much more likely to find the right path, to do the next right thing, to feel better about myself as a person.

I can't stress enough how personal a topic this is. I wouldn't write about it but for the fact that it's been so important to my recovery. Anyone who is trying to work a solid program of recovery will come in contact with faith and spirituality issues. Approach them in a manner you are comfortable with. If you encounter individuals who say you must have a certain type of religion and that it's necessary to practice that religion in a specific way, or else it won't work, my advice is to run away as fast as you can. You'll figure things out on your own. The only requirement is to have an open mind, and if you have questions about something, ask someone you trust.

There are a lot of different religious theories out there. I believe that a few common threads bind them all together: do your best to be a good person; try and do the right things, not only for yourself but for others; be honest with yourself and others. Anyone who can even come close to accomplishing these goals is going to be a pretty good person, a person other people will want to be around, a person with the ability to live with himself.

The basic principles of right and wrong, of good and evil, are within most all of us. I know that I possess the capacity for unbelievable acts of kindness and love. I am also capable of being truly selfish and self-centered at times. When I can approach a situation and take time to ask for guidance, instead of merely reacting to my wants, I'm making an effort to do what is fundamentally right. This pause gives me the opportunity to evaluate the options, and if I'm honest with myself, I can choose to do the right thing. The proper decisions are usually pretty clear. There's no need for debate. When the committee in my head begins to discuss a situation or decision, it's usually a warning sign. When this happens, I have to be very cautious. Most of the time it's my addict brain trying to rationalize a decision in order to convince me I should do something else, something more in line with my will, as opposed to what's right. I may not make the right choice all the time, but no one's perfect. At least I'm trying, and that's what's important.

I never planned on having a spiritual awakening when I decided to quit doing drugs. I'm not even sure if awakening is the right word. For me, it's more of an understanding. It's an understanding that keeps evolving the more I learn and the more I try to implement newfound principles into my life.

Introspection is a big part of recovery, at least for me. Quite frankly, I find it almost unthinkable that anyone could enter into, and remain in, a program of recovery without serious self-examination. After all, it was my problems that brought me to the point where I just had to say, "No more, I've had enough!" It didn't take me long to realize that drugs and alcohol weren't my real problems. They were only the symptoms.

Merely refraining from drug and alcohol use wasn't going to fix my problems. Abstinence might mitigate the overt consequences of my drinking and drugging, but it wasn't going to heal the underlying maladies that fueled my addictions. Unless I address my core problems, I can't change the person I am, the person who drank and drugged. Without change, I would at best be a frightened and insecure person who had problems coping with life. At worst, I would go back out and use in order to dull the pain of living.

My relationship between getting high and enjoying life had blurred to the point where I couldn't enjoy life unless I was high. For most of my adult life I equated having a good time with putting on a good buzz. The reason I had to alter my perception of the world and what was going on around me had nothing to do with the world or what was going on around me. It had to do with me. I wasn't comfortable with life because I wasn't comfortable with me. That's all changed now. My recovery and the steps I've taken to change my life allow me to feel good about myself. I have a sense that I'm becoming the person I always wanted to be but never thought I could be.

April 4, 2007 is the date I began my transition from addiction to sobriety. That was my first day without any alcohol or drugs. The transformation from the person I was to the person I am is a little more difficult to nail down. I think it started pretty early on, when I began attending meetings and listening with an open mind. I heard a lot of ideas and theories on faith and a Higher Power. These topics are staples in most twelve-step recovery meetings. One of the things I really like about these groups, at least the ones that I attend, is that nobody tries to tell me what I have to believe or how my faith should work. What I choose to take from these meetings and incorporate into my life is up to me. What others decide to take from these meetings is up to them, and nobody should tell them differently. If someone tries to impose their beliefs on you, find another meeting. With time and patience, everything will fall into place.

Humility

What is humility? Ask a dozen people and you might get a dozen different answers. That was the case during one of my outpatient sessions. There were a few individuals who drew complete blanks on the subject. I can't remember what my response was. I know that I struggled with it. I know that I responded to the question, although I'm not sure whether my definition accurately described the thoughts I was trying to convey.

I'm always attentive when this topic is brought up in a meeting. I love to hear what people have to say about it. I think it's a very misunderstood concept. In the past I used to think of it as a byproduct of some misdeed or errant behavior. I thought it only surfaced after I had done something wrong. I never viewed it as a characteristic that I should aspire to achieve.

Early in my recovery, I thought my understanding of the term might be incorrect, so I looked it up in the dictionary.

The American Heritage Dictionary defines humility as: (n) "The quality or condition of being humble; lack of pride."

That didn't sound very good. I thought pride was a good thing. Maybe I better check out *humble*.

That same dictionary defines humble as: (adj.) "1. Marked by meekness or modesty in behavior, attitude, or spirit. 2. Showing deferential or submissive respect. 3. Of low rank or station;

unpretentious. (v) 1. To humiliate. 2. To make lower in condition or station."

I was still confused. Was humility good or bad? I like the modesty and unpretentious part. I can understand that—the kind of humility that the MVP player in a championship game would exhibit, when he gives all the credit for the victory to his teammates. I was confused by the verbiage about low rank or station and meekness. Those traits didn't seem to me like very strong characteristics, goals that I should strive for.

Whenever humility was brought up in a meeting during my first few months of recovery, I simply listened. As time went by, I began to grasp the importance of the word. Now I believe it's one of the loftiest goals a person can attain. It may also be one of the most difficult traits to maintain.

I didn't realize it at the time, but humility had been with me since I decided to stop doing drugs and quit drinking. Chemicals had humbled me. Some portions of the above definitions, the less flattering ones, fit me to a tee. I had lost all pride. I was of low rank or station in life. I was meek. I was submissive. I was lost. I was a real-life example of humility and humbleness.

If that's what humility is, why would anyone want to possess it? Wouldn't it be better to be at the top of your field, successful and proud, with the world at your feet? I think it depends. If I can rise to the top and maintain my humility, then that's great. If I make the ascent without humility, I don't think I'll be at the pinnacle for very long. If I lose my humility, it's only a matter of time before I start drinking and drugging again. My shortcomings as a person are what led me down the road of addiction. Without humility, I am unable to shed my shortcomings. Where ego prevented me from acknowledging my shortcomings, humility empowered me to address them.

Furthermore, my character defects will always remain with me. It is only through a continuous effort to work a solid program of recovery that I'm able to keep these personal defects at bay.

Recovery isn't like riding a bike. It's not something you can take classes in and master. Recovery habits, once acquired, must be practiced on a daily basis. If I get complacent and don't continue to grow as a person, I will go backwards. Someone once told me that there's no parking in recovery. You're either moving forward in your recovery, or you are going backwards toward your relapse.

I heard two really good definitions of humility over the past six months. The first one is: humility isn't thinking less of yourself, it's thinking of yourself less. My favorite one is quite simple. To remain teachable is to be humble. As soon as I think I have all the answers, I cease to be humble.

That last sentence is a good indicator of why humility can be so difficult to maintain. As soon as I think I'm starting to get it, I'm apt to become less teachable. As a person, it's important for me to be able to learn and grow every day, as an addict, It's imperative. My sobriety depends on humility. The moment I began to rest on my accomplishments, I'm setting myself up for a fall.

Humility brought me into recovery. Prior to that I was driven by fear. I was afraid to face up to my character defects. It had always been easier for me to bury my problems with drugs and alcohol instead of admitting failure and addressing my flaws. Pride and fear prevented me from admitting I had problems, at least ones that required attention. Flaws translated into weakness, or so I thought. I've always wanted to convey an air of control, the appearance that my life and affairs were in order. I thought that building character was something you did when you were younger. By the time you were an adult, you either had character or you didn't.

Now I realize it's something I can work on every day. Since youth, I've heard the phrase *no one's perfect.* For the most part, I thought that was something you'd say about someone else, not yourself. It's a phrase I would sometimes use as an excuse if I made a mistake, but it wasn't one I wanted to attach to any of my major character traits. In the past, I don't believe I was even honestly aware of all my character defects, let alone how to approach and remedy them. As for the ones I was conscious of, I didn't want to admit them. Doing so would make me look fallible and weak—of a lower rank or station than my peers. That would make me look humble. Not the good humble either, the MVP kind of humility. I'd have the other humble, the one where I didn't measure up, where I had somehow failed.

That's the old me, the one who didn't understand the true meaning of humility. The new me thinks humility is one of the greatest traits an individual can possess. My recognition of its importance in my life continues to grow. At times I have to catch myself. I can be judgmental, just like most inhabitants of this earth. There are times I think I know more than someone else, that my way is the right way. That's the wrong way to practice humility. In these instances, I have a tendency to close my mind and be unreceptive to the thoughts being expressed around me. I'm thinking more of myself than what another person has to say. I'm not being teachable. I'm not being humble. I run the risk of missing out on something that can truly be important, an idea that could benefit me and make my life better. I'm not practicing humility.

Humility keeps me in check. It keeps me in place with my Higher Power. It allows me to stay out of the way, to seek guidance, and to put my Higher Power's will ahead of my will. Humility affords me the opportunity to recognize my character defects and minimize their impact on my life.

Squandering Life's Big Chances

I am faced or presented with opportunities each and every day. Opportunities are funny creatures. They seem to have a chameleon-like quality. Oftentimes they camouflage themselves and can be difficult to spot. They come in all shapes and sizes. If I don't pay attention to what's going on around me, I'm probably going to miss a lot of them.

Some opportunities are recurring, others more infrequent. They may be subject to certain external forces, maybe the weather, geography, and people I surround myself with. If I dig deep and examine this issue, I could probably find a lot of parameters that play a role in determining which opportunities will be available to me at certain times.

I never used to think like this. In the past, I viewed an opportunity as something that would benefit me in some big way. A lot of times the opportunities would be financial in nature More than likely they would in some way involve material possessions— the opportunity to make a deal or forge a new alliance that would somehow put more coins in my pocket: a stock tip, a new client, acquiring something for less than fair market value. I used to feel that for a situation to be a true opportunity, I must benefit with something that was tangible, something I could put my hands on, usually something of monetary value. Such situations were what I defined as opportunities. I would tell myself that I was macro, a big-picture person. I would wait for opportunities to appear, hoping they would just fall into my lap or be given to me. Oftentimes it was necessary to perform a risk/reward analysis. Maybe the payoff wasn't big enough, and the risk wasn't worth taking a chance on.

I don't know exactly when, but my thinking has shifted from these old views. Now I look for opportunities in the little things that, in the past, would have seemed so mundane, so boring, and so insignificant. Here's an example. It's about as simple as it gets: the opportunity to enjoy an hour of solitude, of peacefulness, some time to reflect, or just enjoy what's going on around me. It doesn't necessarily have to be an hour; sometimes five minutes is all I need. Sometimes five minutes is all that's available. An hour would be nice, but if it's not on the menu, I guess I'll have the five-minute special.

How about the opportunity to talk to someone special in your life, a family member or close friend, someone you haven't spoken with in a while? Even if you spoke with that person yesterday, it's okay to connect with them again today, even if it's just a hello, just to let them know you're thinking about them.

I'm finding out that if I'm proactive, I have the ability to create opportunities. Quite frequently, these opportunities boil down to nothing more than making a choice, a better choice than I would have made in the past. I'm beginning to view each day as a canvas, an opportunity to paint whatever picture I choose for the day. I've transformed from an almost vegetative state, one in which I sat or lay around waiting for things to happen, to one in which I realize that I can, to a large extent, shape each day as it fits me.

I must always keep in mind that I am powerless over people, places, and things, but that's not a problem. I can add these things to my canvas. Maybe the day's rendering will be a paint-by-numbers portrait, where the people, places, and things comprise some of the numbers, or pigments, that will be used in the picture. Nonetheless, I have the freedom to work with these numbers, to use my own personal brushstrokes and apply the colors. Even if I have to work around certain challenges and obstacles in my day, I have a lot of control over what I can do and how I can do it. I like to paint now, to be productive. I'm a different person.

Who we are at any given time and space is always changing, even if it's nothing more than the sweep of the second hand on the clock. We're older, even if only by a matter of seconds. Life is fluid. The world keeps moving. I may choose to be stagnant, but the world, life itself, refuses to remain stationary. It continues to keep on keeping on.

I've been talking about small opportunities, or at least that's the way they might appear. What about the big ones? Are they recognizable? Are they predictable? How can I be prepared to grasp the next big one? My advice would be to grasp the little ones, the ones that are around us every day. If I can do that, I really feel confident that when the next big one comes along, I'll be ready to seize it.

More important is the fact that if I can maintain this attitude and live my life by these simple guidelines, I'm already taking full advantage of the biggest opportunity ever placed in my lap. It's one that everyone has the ability to achieve: simply living and enjoying life. Enjoy each and every day. Make your opportunities. Make the little choices that enrich each day. After all, it's the quality of life that's important. Quantity is just a bonus. I'm not sure what the point of life is if there's no quality.

The quality of my life is proportional to my capacity to appreciate the little things around me. My ability to appreciate and be grateful is dependent on my sobriety. I'm given the opportunity to stay sober on a daily basis. This opportunity has always been there, I just never recognized it, at least not for what it was and what it had to offer. Now that I am aware of the tremendous rewards that sobriety can afford me, I have no intention of squandering them. There's no risk for me either, not really. I had a feeling in my early days of sobriety that I was sacrificing something. I thought I was passing up an opportunity by not getting high, but I had it backwards. I created opportunities by changing my old behavior.

I suppose there is a trade-off there. I've given up the opportunity to drink socially, to enjoy the occasional glass of wine. But the benefits of sobriety so greatly outweigh the costs, there's no question of what I should choose. That's just me, though. It's a decision that everyone must make for himself. The great thing, however, is that you can always go back if you need to. Alcohol and drugs will always be there. If I ever get to the point where I don't think it's worth it, being sober, I can go back out. For now, I choose to take advantage of this opportunity, one day at a time.

Working With Others

Alcoholics and addicts have a unique gift. It's an endowment that usually can't be realized or tapped into until an individual embarks on some type of program of recovery. Our curse can become a blessing. We have the ability to help other addicts and alcoholics where all others have failed. Our experiences have benefited us with an education that can't be learned in school. We can relate to others in our fraternity at a level that those not afflicted with the disease will be unable to comprehend. We can be successful where all others have failed.

It usually makes little if any difference what our drug of choice was. To most of our kind, a drug is a drug, be it alcohol or cocaine, heroin or pot, uppers or downers. It's not so important what we put in our bodies, it's what happens to our bodies after we put the substance into our system, the decisions we make and the actions we take.

There are still some alcoholics out there who think they're better than addicts, and there are some addicts who think they're somehow different from alcoholics. I got news for anyone of this opinion: we are the same. You may think that you're different, but your disease doesn't. Your life is being controlled by a chemical substance. Your addiction doesn't care whether you get your stuff from a liquor store or on a street corner. Either way, the end result will be the same.

We have all shared very similar experiences throughout the course of our addictions. This fact becomes very obvious when we become involved in a program of recovery. It doesn't matter whether we're attending an inpatient treatment facility or going to outside twelve-step meetings. We all share the same problems. We all share the same pain. That's one of the reasons the bond between the members of a support group is so strong.

The singularity of purpose behind these groups allows individuals from all stations of life to come together and do their best to help one another. When principals are placed ahead of personalities, amazing results are possible and tremendous rewards can be reaped.

Early in my journaling, before I even thought of beginning this project, a few things happened that had a tremendous impact on me. I always wanted to be a writer, to have something I created published and made available to the public. What a testament that would be to my time here on earth.

I can tell you that this project is not what I envisioned as my literary debut. Where's the intrigue and irony? What about the hero and the villain? All I was doing was journaling, recording my feelings and observations on a daily basis. It was a tool to help me cope with early sobriety. Writing helped me solidify concepts and ideas I was learning about in my outpatient sessions and at my twelve-step recovery meetings. I didn't pay much attention to whether my fledgling ideas regarding sobriety were good or bad, right or wrong. All I knew was they were helping me stay sober, one day at time. As a result of my work, I began to gain a better understanding of what would be required of me in order to not only maintain my sobriety but to be happy in my sobriety as well.

Some recovery groups may be more structured than others, but the basic principles are the same. We share our experiences and work on the present: how we're feeling, what we're doing right, and what we are doing wrong. If we're in a bad place, how do we get out of it, and if we find ourselves in a good place, how can we stay there? What do we need to work on going forward that will make our lives better? What actions are necessary so we don't drink or use today?

About halfway through my IOP program, I received a call one evening. It was late, and I was getting ready for bed, so I almost didn't take the call. It was someone from my group, and he was having a few problems. Any apprehension I may have felt about fielding a call so late evaporated less than a minute into the conversation. My new friend told me that he liked what I had to say in group and that my comments helped him. He was having some problems and needed someone to talk to.

I'm no Dr. Phil. I'm just an addict with a drinking problem, or a drunk who did too many drugs, take your pick. We chatted for twenty or thirty minutes, nothing profound. We talked about our problems and our fears. I helped him and he helped me. At the end of the conversation we both felt better. He had a better understanding of the situations that were troubling him, and I had gained my first glimpse of what it feels like to truly be of service to someone else, someone in need. It was then, and still is today, an amazing feeling.

This wasn't the first time I'd helped someone or done something for somebody. Most of us do things for other people all the time. Sometimes it's personal and sometimes professional. I'm an attorney. Every client I ever served was either burdened with some sort of problem or had something that needed fixed. Those situations were different. My services were expected; they were part of my job. Most of the time, I was paid for my services. There was still a sense of accomplishment involved, but it was a different feeling. It wasn't the same as performing a selfless act, something that is not required, an action that is offered solely for the benefit of another.

In the past, I worked on the board of a local charity for a few years, and I've handled my share of pro bono cases as an attorney.

These are the closest experiences I've had to working with other addicts and alcoholics. There is, however, one big difference between the two situations. When I work with someone who suffers from my disease, it helps me stay sober. In that respect, I'm not really performing a selfless act.

Working with others is a big part of my recovery program. It's a big part of any twelve-step recovery program. There are some who believe it is the most important part of a program. That may be true. Most certainly, without service to others, there would be no twelve-step programs.

I have an obligation to be there for someone who is suffering and needs my help. The hands of those who came before me were stretched out to help pull me up when I was down. Those hands, and the bodies and hearts they're attached to, are there for me every day, 24/7.

I have new friends, whom I've known for less than six months, that I can call any hour of the day if I have a problem. Unlike a lot of people I've known in the past, some of whom I've called friends, these new acquaintances ask nothing of me, nothing but to be of assistance, and that I be there for them should they need me. It's a symbiotic relationship.

There's a certain mentality among addicts and alcoholics, some invisible attraction that draws us together. When I was using, I tended to run with others who shared my same interests, those who enjoyed drinking and getting high. We all had something in common. In sobriety, I still hang around with addicts and alcoholics. The only difference between now and then is that now, we have a desire to abstain from alcohol and drugs. We're still alcoholics and addicts. We still think the same. We're just trying to move in a different direction than we did in the past. We use the same mentality that used to get us high to try to keep us clean.

There's a big difference between hanging out with people who used to drink and drug, as opposed to people who never drank or used. Both groups may be sober, but they're like night and day. There's a difference between knowing how not to do something and knowing how to stop doing something.

Someone who's learned how to stop doing something can help me do the same, whereas someone who's never done something won't know where to start. That's why I have new friends, ones who can help me with my journey, ones who know where I've been and where I want to go. It doesn't matter how much sobriety people have. They may have a couple days, a couple months, a couple years, or many years. Regardless of how much time they have, they have something that can help me.

When I see someone with a lot of sobriety, someone who's really living life on life's terms, it encourages me. I want to be able to achieve the same comfort with myself and the world around me. When I'm with someone who's just come in, someone who only has a few days clean, it reminds me where I once was and of the places I don't want to return to. I find strength in both situations. There's no real hierarchy in the system, either. We all help one another, regardless of time clean. The new can help the old, just as the old can help the new. It's a pretty neat situation, one that's hard to find in other areas of life.

I have the ability to help people every day, and it's really not that difficult. Usually all I have to do is listen to them and share their burden. I have to remember that I'm powerless over other people. I can't make others happy when they're sad. I can't make them peaceful when they're angry. Most of the time all I can do is listen to them and maybe offer some advice.

Regardless of whether I'm successful in helping them, I'm helping myself on these occasions. Simply by making the effort to be of service to someone, I'm serving myself as well. When I'm trying to be of service to another human being, I'm practicing humility without even realizing it. It's tough to think of yourself when you're trying to work on someone else's problems.

It's also very rewarding when you are able to help someone who's battling a life-threatening disease like addiction and alcoholism. I'm not only helping that person, I'm helping everyone around him. I'm helping his family, his spouse and children, his parents and siblings. I have the ability to affect everyone around that person, through that person. If he feels better, the effects may trickle down to everyone he comes in contact with, and so on and so on, until the number of people I've touched is uncountable.

I don't have to limit my humanitarian efforts to addicts and alcoholics. In fact, I try not to. Even though I was a nice guy when I was getting high, I'm still an addict, and addicts are selfish. The simple reality of the disease is that it was more important to feed my habit than to help those around me. Even though I was almost completely isolated for quite a while, I'm sure I could've done more on those rare occasions when I did leave the house.

Just think about that trickle-down effect I talked about above. Every act of kindness that I perform has the potential to affect an untold number of people. Simply making someone smile or feel good for a few minutes is all it takes. That person may pass that positive energy on to the next person he encounters. I know it's happened to me before: someone has done something for me, and I feel so good that I do something nice for the next person I bump into. Even if the effort doesn't get passed on, at least I've done something for another human being.

I think it's quite easy for human beings to get hung up on the big picture. For the most part, people would like to make the world a better place. So often these plans involve grandiose, larger-than-life proposals. Most of us think we are powerless to make changes, that we're too insignificant in the grand scheme of things. Just because an individual may not have the ability to cut greenhouse gases and single-handedly save the ozone layer doesn't mean that person can't make the world a better place.

Making the world a better place is easy. We do it all the time and probably don't even realize it. Every time we do something positive for another human being, we make the world a better place.

Life Is a Full-Time Job

Since I've been in recovery, I've noticed that I always have something to do, or at least there is something I should be doing. There really isn't a lot of downtime. I've been working pretty hard on my life lately. It's a good hard, a rewarding hard. At times I feel a little guilty.

I have to be honest. When someone compliments me for what I'm doing, the way I am trying to turn my life around, I don't know what to think, let alone what to say. I'm just doing my job, the job at hand, staying sober. I'm just trying to do the right thing, maintaining a lifestyle, that I assume the majority of the population is doing successfully, on a daily basis.

Living is a full-time job. Even when I try to back off, to take it easy, there's still work to do. Not necessarily manual labor or slaving away at the office, but there're things to do. I still have decisions to make, and unless I'm home alone or taking a nap, I have to interact with other people. There's always something around the house I can do: laundry, dishes, bills, hobbies and projects, reading, writing, or simply taking care of the basic chores that life leaves in its path. There's always something to do.

I used to avoid a lot of the things that are now part of my daily routine. When I was getting high, I was working full time, it's just that my efforts weren't producing anything that was beneficial. Most people looking in from the outside can't even begin to comprehend how much effort was involved in staying high all the time. Maintaining a constant supply of drugs is very difficult. When you are smoking them, there is always something to do: prepare the drugs, clean the pipes, buy supplies, etc., etc. If I wasn't at home getting high, I was running around somewhere seeing to all the duties involved with staying high. It wasn't glamorous, nor was it productive. Nonetheless, it was a full-time job.

I guess my point is, regardless of whether I am doing the wrong thing or the right thing, either way, life's a full-time job. I used to think it was easy to do the wrong thing, that there wasn't much effort involved. I was wrong. Now when I look back on those old days, I'm amazed at the amount of effort and risk I was able to cram into a twenty-four-hour period. Most addicts will find that if they are able to put as much effort into their daily endeavors at sobriety as they did to support their addictions, they can accomplish more than they ever imagined.

It's a great feeling to go to bed at night and know that I had a great day, a productive day. I do a lot of little things on a daily basis that in the past I would've completely avoided, or at least put off until they became absolutely necessary, simple things like picking up, doing laundry, cleaning the kitchen or my office. I used to hate doing these things. I'm not saying I love to do them now, it's just that I don't mind them as much these days. I do like the feeling at the end of the day of having been able to knock down some of these domestic chores.

Most of my aversion to day-to-day responsibilities is my addict brain telling me I don't want to do something or that I don't like to do something, as opposed to any genuine dislike for the activity. More often than not, as soon as I start a project, I realize it's not really that bad. Furthermore, it usually takes no time at all to complete the task. Laziness, selfishness, and a poor thinker are a bad combination. I had those bases covered when I was using.

Keeping busy is important to me for another reason. It's dangerous for an addict or alcoholic to get bored. How many times in the past did I tell myself that since there was nothing going on, I might as well get high? Even before I became a full-blown addict, any gap in my schedule was a great excuse to use drugs or alcohol to fill the void. If I was meeting people for dinner and I got to the restaurant early, I'd have some drinks. When I was traveling, if I got to the airport before time to board the plane, I'd have some drinks. If I was sitting around with nothing to do, might as well go to a bar and have some drinks. Drinking was always a good space-filler for me, more so than drugs. That's probably because drinking is a more socially acceptable way to pass time.

I spend a lot of time working on my recovery. In one respect, I'm always working on it, twenty-four hours a day, trying to implement principles and practices into my daily affairs. I also try to earmark at least a couple of hours a day for meetings. A lot of newcomers to recovery balk at the idea of allocating that much time to their program. I know I did, after my first rehab. Part of the reason for my reluctance was that I didn't understand the importance of these meetings and the impact they would have on my recovery. Initially, I thought they were a waste of time. I had things to do. Those crazy counselors couldn't seriously expect me to devote that much time out of my busy schedule to some silly meetings.

One of the points that both my inpatient and IOP counselors stressed was that taking a little time out of my day for a meeting was nothing compared to the amount of time I wasted on my addiction. Well, duh! Yeah, okay, but partying is fun and meetings are boring. That's how I used to think, but not anymore. The counselors' wisdom holds true for me, as I'm sure it does for just about every addict and alcoholic out there. Even before I got all messed up, when I was going to work regularly, when I was living what I thought was a pretty normal life, I still managed to devote a couple hours a day to drinking and partying.

I make time for my meetings, plain and simple. By the time I got to IOP, my counselors didn't have to convince me. By then, I knew it was the right thing to do. More importantly, it was something I wanted to do. It got to the point where I really got a kick out of listening to other group members' excuses for not attending any outside twelve-step recovery meetings.

When an addict or an alcoholic begins treatment, it's amazing how busy and hectic their schedules get. All the responsibilities and obligations they used to shirk are suddenly first and foremost on their daily list of things to do. I understand it. That's the way our brains work: denial and rationalization. It's all part of the misconception that all we have to do is quit, and everything will be okay.

There are those out there who can just stop using or drinking on their own; fortunately I'm not one of them. I almost wrote, *unfortunately,* I'm not one of them. Five or six months ago, I would've written that. I don't feel that way anymore. Maybe I'm just one of those who needed a lot of fixing, but I've learned so much from my twelve-step meetings and the people who attend them. I truly am fortunate. I have a totally different approach to life than the one I used to stumble through with for the last thirty years or so.

Taking drugs and alcohol out of my life freed up a lot of my time. Meetings were, and still are, a great way to fill some of the void. The hours I devote to my meetings are one of the most important and beneficial ways for me to utilize my time. The education I get from attending them helps me keep and enjoy all the wonderful things in my life, all the things I have been blessed with.

There are twenty-four hours in a day; that's a constant. What I choose to do with that time is up to me. When I was making the wrong choices, time seemed to fly by, so long as I didn't run out of supplies. Days would just seem to disappear. The problem was, I never got anything accomplished. On those occasions when I ran out of drugs, when I was waiting to get resupplied, I would be paralyzed. It was as though the second hand on the clock stopped moving, as if time were standing still. I was completely useless when this happened. I was less productive when I ran out of drugs than when I had them.

These days, when I'm trying to make the right decisions, I'm still faced with the same twenty-four hours in a day. Time still flies by. It seems to evaporate in two- and three-hour chunks. I'm usually up and writing before the sun sees the sky. Before I realize it, it's midmorning, and my son's awake. On some days I'll hit a morning meeting or a noon meeting, sometimes both. Next stop, midafternoon, and before I know it, it's time to eat dinner. It's common for me to look back and wonder where my day went. Oftentimes I won't be able to account for the recently departed hours of that day, but in their wake, I'll find a list of accomplishments that serve as testimony that I had a productive day. A lot of times, I don't get to everything I intend to. That's okay, so long as I do the best I can. My measuring rod is my ability to go to bed each night knowing that I had a good day. It's a great gauge, as long as I'm honest with myself. At the end of the day, I know what I've accomplished, and I know what I could have accomplished. I'm the only one I have to impress or answer to. It makes no difference what anyone else thinks or says to me. As long as I'm satisfied with my daily production, that's all that matters.

Either way, life's a full-time job. It just took me a while to realize that the pay's better when I do things the right way.

Life Isn't Fair

I've heard this said countless times. I've uttered the phrase on numerous occasions. I've thought about it too many times to remember. Whether it's true or not, I don't know. It's beyond my capacity to determine whether life is fair. There was a time when I would dwell on this notion for endless hours, when it would haunt me for days, weeks, sometimes even months.

What I do know is that regardless of the amount of mental energy I put into answering this age-old question, at the end of the day, I'll probably be no closer to resolving the riddle than when I first began pondering it. I'm trying to take a different tack on the issue these days. Instead of worrying whether I'm getting a fair shake, or a just roll of the dice, I'm just trying to do what is right. Do the right thing and get out of the way. Let others judge whether or not things are fair. After all, I can't do anything about it, and getting angry or developing resentment over something won't change anything.

It's probably safe to say that some events in life aren't fair. That doesn't mean that life, overall, isn't fair. Maybe life is like a sporting event; there are good calls, and bad calls. Sometimes things go my way, other times they don't, but in the end it all equals out. So far, I think most of the decisions are going my way, but even if they're not, there's not a whole lot I can do about it. Unlike sporting events, there's no instant replay, and there are no officials who can huddle up, have a conference, and reverse a call. I'm on my own when it comes to dealing with how events transpired in my life.

Of course, if some grave injustice is perpetrated upon me, I can always seek redress through the courts. But even if I am successful, it won't change the fact that I was wronged, that I was treated unfairly. Sometimes my first instinct is to take matters into my own hands and right the wrong through my own actions. If I do this, I run the risk of not only hurting someone else but of escalating the situation and making things worse for me.

I'm learning that it's usually better to put things behind me and move on with my life. In retrospect, many of the events in my life that I initially perceived as being unfair have turned out to be important milestones in my journey to where I am today. Adversity has proven to be a very competent instructor. It's important for me to be able to deal with life when things don't go my way. Without bad breaks, it would be very difficult, if not impossible, for me to deal with life's downturns.

What about being fair when I'm dealing with others? The best I can do is try to be fair to myself and those around me. This, coupled with doing the right thing, is the key for me. I think that if I do the right thing, or at least make my best effort, fairness will take care of itself, somehow, some way. Maybe situations won't play out exactly as I had scripted them in my head, but however they turn out is most likely how they are supposed to be.

When I look at life, and the decisions I make, most of the time my actions are going to affect others in some way. When I make a decision and take action, I start a chain reaction, one that I have no control over. Maybe somewhere along the line someone will be affected unfavorably because of something I've done, fair or unfair. I can't do anything about it.

Therefore, the best way for me to cope with this is to try and do the next right thing. Then, whatever the outcome, I can at least be comforted by the fact that I was doing the best I possibly could. What's fair, or at least what I perceive to be fair, might not end up being fair to someone else. A lot of times what's right and what's fair may be the same thing; other times it won't.

I need to concentrate on doing what's right. What's fair is a judgment call. No matter how hard I try, it can be difficult to be 100 percent impartial. That's why our judicial system has a process for the recusal of judges from certain cases, and why surgeons don't operate on family members. If I can stick to what's right and make amends when I'm wrong, fairness will take care of itself.

I won't know for sure whether life has been fair to me until my time on this earth is over. I've got a sneaking suspicion that, all in all, it will be. In the event that this prediction is wrong, I'll find myself in the same situation I find myself now: unable to do anything about it.

Status Check

This is a bit of a deviation from my usual routine. Other than my journal entries, I haven't tried to write a piece on how I'm feeling at any given moment. These next few pages are intended to be a snapshot of where my head's at.

I have been walking around Los Angeles for about forty-five minutes. I'm at Melrose and Stanley (7600 block), and I need a break. I was lucky enough to find a Starbucks. I just sat down on the patio. I've got some issues that are eating at me. I've been trying to work them out all morning. The more I think about my day, the better this concept seems. Just empty my head, and get it all on paper.

I've been writing about all these new ideas and tools that I'm trying to apply to my life in order to make me a better, happier person. The main reason I want to write something about my day and how I'm feeling is that it struck me that if you're reading this book, you may be getting the impression that I have everything figured out, that I have discovered the secret to life. Even though I have a pretty good idea of the direction I want my life to go, that doesn't mean things are wonderful all the time.

I have some issues with my wife, and they are making it very difficult for me to stay in the moment and keep myself centered. I'm upset. I'm having a hard time enjoy everything going on around me. Just about everything I have been writing about is bubbling up and beating the crap out of me: resentment, anger, expectations, acceptance, doing the next right thing, pretty much everything. I've been disturbed over some of the things she has said and done over the past few days. I find myself dwelling on the stuff, and it starts sucking me back into the past, to many of the problems I have tried to put behind me. It's causing me to project out into the future, to manufacture new problems and concerns, things that haven't yet and may never happen. I've tried pausing, not reacting, focusing on the good around me, and preparing a gratitude list.

Guess what? It's getting better. I'm not completely satisfied at this moment, but I'm a lot happier than I would have been in the past, given my current circumstances. I haven't even come close to a total emotional meltdown. What this tells me is that this stuff works. My wife is who she is. I love her. I don't agree, nor do I accept some of the things she does, but I'm sure the feelings are mutual with her as well.

I think that's it. There will always be problems, but life is much more manageable now. Life isn't perfect. It can only be as good as I am willing to let it be. Even if I fight, kick, scratch, and claw, I'll still end up right where I am. I'm going to do the best I can and see where that leads me.

I wrote the above thoughts about two and a half months into sobriety. I celebrate six months of sobriety on Thursday, three days from now. The incident in L.A. was the first time I was genuinely challenged, when my new lifestyle was really put to the test. I've been tested many times since then. The outcome is always the same. Everything always works out. I don't get as upset as I used to, and when things do go wrong, I'm able to snap out of my funk a lot quicker. I find myself smiling at a lot of things that used to irritate me. On top of all this, I really haven't had a serious compulsion to drink or use drugs.

During the first three or four months of my sobriety, I would get worried when I let something bother me. I felt as if I wasn't doing something right. I had this misconception that if I did everything I was supposed to, I wasn't going to have any problems. Now I realize that problems are a part of life. What's important is how I respond to them and how I let them affect me.

I am learning how to live life on life's terms. I used to think I was living my life on *my* terms. My way was a recipe for disaster. I don't know where I ever got the idea that I could call the shots. Life doesn't give a damn about who you are, how much money you have, or who your family and friends are. Life's got a plan of its own. Life is going to win. I can either get on board, or I can get run over. Getting run over is no fun. I tried it for a long time.

I've got a chance now. I'm learning how to cope with all that life has to throw at me. In the past, I only had one way to deal with life, one tool, and that was alcohol and drugs. They worked for a while. I was able to either avoid or slide through some troubling situations. I was never truly able to address or solve the problems, but I got through them. Unfortunately, there were also a lot of side effects associated with this course of action.

Now I have a brand new toolbox full of new tools. I'm still learning how to use them. Like most things in life, a little practice goes a long way. I'm getting better at handling the tools every day. Some days they're really user friendly, and other days I have to be very patient and take my time with them.

I've touched on quite a few topics throughout the course of these materials. I've covered the important areas, the ones that helped me transition from an active state of addiction to my current place in sobriety. Until recently, I was worried I might state something incorrectly or somehow make a mistake in my presentation of these materials. But I realized that I can't make a mistake so long as I'm honest with my assessment of my situation: where I was and what I've done to get to where I am today. I'm never going to have all the answers, not for me or anybody else. This project isn't supposed to be an overview and instruction manual from someone with years and years of sobriety and experience. If that was the case I wouldn't be the one writing it. I'm new at this, but if you're new at this too, maybe some of the materials in this book can help you.

It's not always easy, but it doesn't have to always be difficult, either. I know that for me, I just have to take it one day at a time. Regardless of what's going on around me, it's always up to me to decide how I'm going to feel. It's my choice and no one else's. I can choose to be happy or I can choose to be sad. That's it, no less, no more. Of course, I could substitute another adverb for sad, to describe how I'm feeling, or how I'm going to choose to feel. I can be angry, depressed, jealous, resentful, apathetic, spiteful, morose, pessimistic, or just plain miserable.

I'm well aware that it's both physically and emotionally impossible for me to just decide that I'm going to be happy all the time, 24/7, 365 days a year. I'm a human being, the most complex piece of equipment on the face of the earth. I'm going to have some down time. My goal, however, is to try and minimize the amount of time that I'm in the shop, getting repairs, fixing myself up after my last mental fender bender with that certain someone who always seems to get my goat.

Having a choice is a big deal to me. In the past, I never thought I had a choice about how I was going to feel on a lot of occasions. I thought I was supposed to let the situation dictate how I was going to feel at any given time. Big surprise! It's all up to me, and it's all up to you too. Excuse me, your life is waiting. Good luck!